Praise for *Brilliant Headteacher*

'One of the first books on the role of Headteacher which hasn't become lost in the mire of academic musings about the job and doesn't simply report the findings of academics who are no longer or may never have been Headteachers themselves! A practical guide to Headship has been long needed and this book might be the definitive guide. A well-structured and practical guide to Headship which allows a busy Headteacher to dip in and out for support, guidance and advice when it is needed the most – when difficulties arise!

Marc Bowen, Deputy Headteacher

'A worthwhile text for every Head and potential Head...conveys so many of the truths of headship'.

Mick Waters, Professor of Education and President of the Curriculum Foundation

'… an ideal read for anyone considering becoming a Headteacher and/ or beginning the application process.'

Angela Matthews, Senior Teacher

Brilliant series list

Harcombe: *Brilliant Primary School Teacher*
Torn and Bennett: *Brilliant Secondary School Teacher*
Bowen: *Brilliant Subject Leader*
Bunrham: *Brilliant Teaching Assistant*
Smith: *Brilliant Trainee Teacher*

brilliant headteacher

What you need to know to be a truly outstanding headteacher

Iain Erskine

Prentice Hall
is an imprint of

Harlow, England • London • New York • Boston • San Francisco • Toronto • Sydney • Singapore • Hong Kong
Tokyo • Seoul • Taipei • New Delhi • Cape Town • Madrid • Mexico City • Amsterdam • Munich • Paris • Milan

PEARSON EDUCATION LIMITED

Edinburgh Gate
Harlow CM20 2JE
Tel: +44 (0)1279 623623
Fax: +44 (0)1279 431059
Website: www.pearsoned.co.uk

First published in Great Britain in 2011

ISBN: 978-0-273-73594-6

British Library Cataloguing-in-Publication Data
A catalogue record for this book is available from the British Library

Library of Congress Cataloging-in-Publication Data
A catalog record for this book is available from the Library of Congress

10 9 8 7 6 5 4 3 2 1
15 14 13 12 11

Typeset in 10/14pt Plantin by 3
Printed and bound in Great Britain by Henry Ling Ltd., at the Dorset Press,
Dorchester, Dorset

This book is dedicated to my wonderfully supportive family and all the staff and colleagues that I have worked with over the years. But significantly it is dedicated to the children, the pupils and the students that have enriched my life by simply being themselves.

Contents

About the author

Iain Erskine is Head of Fulbridge School and Children's Centre, a 700-place primary school, with 0–2, 2–3 and 3–4 nursery classes; there are about 130 adults working in the school in all the different capacities. The school is situated in a deprived area of Peterborough that has been accurately described by Ofsted as being rich in social and cultural diversity. The school has children from over 30 different nationalities and in recent years has admitted a significant number of Eastern European children.

Iain has been in teaching for 35 years, 15 of them as a Headteacher. He started as a secondary school PE teacher and became a Head of Department before moving into the primary sector and becoming a Deputy Head and Head of an Infant School, and then being appointed to his current post as Head of Fulbridge Primary School. He was also a Primary PE advisor for Cambridgeshire.

He has been through four Ofsted inspections and two years of intensive Special Measures inspections after taking on a school six months into the Special Measures process. He has worked in three secondary schools and five primary schools.

Iain led a Peterborough initiative involving 25 schools, called Oasis, to develop a relevant, creative and innovative curriculum that is based on first-hand experiences that develop the whole child, aspiring to make children into creative thinkers and learners. He has worked with the Qualifications and Curriculum Authority on a unique residential conference for children to look at what, in their eyes, 'makes learning worth it'.

His current school provides an exciting and varied curriculum with themed corridors and classrooms, recreated into 'museum-like' role-play areas to support and inspire the children's love of learning.

Iain took over the Junior School when it was in Special Measures. It was a very old-fashioned school with quality of teaching, management/leadership and very disruptive behaviour identified as the main issues to address. The school has been transformed and in 2004 amalgamated with the neighbouring Infant School to become a Primary School.

Iain has taught children from the ages of 5–18 but was never brave enough to teach in Reception with the 4–5 year olds; still not a bad track record for a secondary school PE teacher! He has dealt with redundancy situations, Special Measures, dismissal of staff, capability procedures, the death of a much-loved colleague, challenging and successful Ofsted Inspections as well as the highs of good SATs results. His drive for the school to take on creativity as the basis of its curriculum approach led him into presenting seminars all over the country in colleges of further education and local and national conferences (including the Education Show and the National Schools of Creativity Conference), to the Heads and staff in Guernsey schools as well as at the London Institute of Education. He talks about his experiences as a Head and developing a 'Creative Curriculum in a Creative Environment'. In fact it was after one such seminar at the annual Education Show in Birmingham that he was approached to write this book.

In 2005 the Ofsted team described Iain as an inspirational Head, gave a glowing report and said they saw no evidence of bad behaviour. SATs scores remain a challenge but are now above national averages and in 2009 and 2010 the CVA (contextual value added) from KS1 to end of KS2 in mathematics put the school in the top 10% of schools nationally for CVA. The significant improvements are undoubtedly down to the changes in the curriculum and the way the school is now managed and led.

In 2009 his school became a National School of Creativity; one of only 56 schools nationally from all educational sectors to gain this status from Creative Partnerships.

Born in 1954, Iain is married, with three sons. Education dominates the family's life. His wife is a Higher Level Teaching Assistant (HLTA), one son is a teacher, one is a Personal Trainer, Sports Coach and HLTA for Sport in a school, and the youngest is studying English at university and has so far avoided a life in education!

Acknowledgements

A school's curriculum should be based on the needs of the children, and its community based on their collective schemata, the sum of all their experiences. In writing this book, which draws upon my experiences in education, it is only right to acknowledge the people who have influenced me and hence this book as part of my educational schemata. It is hard to have original ideas, the trick is to be a lifelong learner and poach as many ideas as you can!

I have attended National College annual leadership conferences each year and the world-renowned speakers they attract have inspired me and have made an impact upon my educational practice and hence the content of this book. From my perspective, the work and ideas of Mick Waters in particular have influenced many of my practices and approaches in school to do with curriculum and leadership. The writings, thoughts and presentations of other educationalists like Sir Ken Robinson and Sir Tim Brighouse have affected me and millions of other educationalists because of their wonderful ideas, analysis and common sense. Tim Brighouse's short books, *The Jigsaw of a Successful School* and *How Successful Headteachers Survive and Thrive* are a wonderful summary of the factors that make an effective school leader.

I must also acknowledge the helpfulness of the EPM (Education Personnel Management) in Huntingdon, Peterborough Local Authority, Ofsted and DCSF websites that have helped me get my facts right!

Closer to home Roger Cole, a national advisor, has had a significant impact on my thinking and practice and started my journey towards a creative approach to the curriculum, and his ideas are still evident all round our school. Mathilda Joubert, another highly respected advisor and educationalist, influenced my and the staff's views of good curriculum practice enormously and Di Goldsmith, who managed our local network of schools, Oasis, and based herself in our school, guided much of the learning journey that the school and I have taken. I would also like to acknowledge the support of the Leadership Team in my current school and in particular the Deputy Heads, Caroline Dingle and Charlotte Krzanicki. Caroline has been extremely active in supporting and contributing to the writing of this book and a school governor, Michael Henchman, has helped enormously with proof reading the book and offering an independent view of its content. Finally if you are lucky enough, as I am, to have an outstanding Chair of Governors, in a lady called Helen Bath, you have to acknowledge the hugely positive impact that such a person can have on your professional life.

Publisher's acknowledgements

We are grateful to the following for permission to reproduce copyright material:

Peterborough City Council for material from the Peterborough City Council Governor's Handbook in Chapter 6 (please contact the council directly for the most up-to-date information available); Figure 10.1 from 'Big Picture of the Curriculum', The Qualifications and Curriculum Development Agency (www. qcda.gov.uk); Crown Copyright material is reproduced with permission under the terms of the Click-use license.

In some instances we have been unable to trace the owners of copyright material, and we would appreciate any information that would enable us to do so.

Foreword

There are quite a few brilliant Headteachers about, always have been. Yet defining one is difficult. Descriptions vary; there are so many different facets that everyone sees a different angle on the same role. Parents see one face, children a slightly different one, staff, Governors, other Headteachers yet another. And then there are the media, Ofsted, School Improvement Partners and all manner of other stakeholders. No wonder the same person wears so many different hats. So, what makes a brilliant Headteacher?

This engaging book draws out the complexity of the modern day role of headship. Brilliant Heads usually have the capacity to work with the whole range of interest groups. They have usually grown into the role through good formal training, good experiences in other schools, and they have more often than not got a good support system inside their school and out.

They are usually strategic and have a set of fundamental principles around which they lead their school community. Their principles are firmly held beliefs which are not the parroting of a nationally driven set of frameworks but a clear view which takes advantage of what is there nationally within the local context of their school.

Brilliant Heads are good with people. They build a team and recognise that success means addressing matters and dealing with difficulties as well as enjoying the easy days. This book dwells on how teams are built, what we do when things get rough, and how we hold to a common vision.

Of course, good Headteachers have to get the underlying business done: the budget, the building, the development plans and the SEF. These are all the bureaucracy of modern headship that the management speakers would have us believe create effectiveness. They need doing well by someone and good Headteachers get them done well and check they are correct. They align these tasks to making learning better rather than making sure that they are playing offices and enjoying the secretarial success.

At the heart of it all, though, brilliant Headteachers hold dear to one thing: effective learning. They know what it is both in experience and outcome for the pupil. They can explain it. They endlessly read about what is going on elsewhere, study research into learning and capitalise on what we now know about the brain and how it operates. They can promote a vision that others can understand and they are clear in their decisions in making them relate to the learning priorities agreed. They don't compromise, accept double standards, or run the institution for the staff or the parents. They sacrifice all else for the learning that they so value for their pupils.

In this book, Iain Erskine outlines why headship is the best job in the world. What we do know is that it is a changing world. Technology, connectedness, fast-paced lives, climate change, sustainability, the gap between rich and poor and the shift of people around the globe create a different context for learning from even 20 years ago. Children have to learn different things nowadays; they need a range of personal qualities and skills that set them fair for a future of uncertainty and promise. The Headteacher who can manage that against a backdrop of the traditional, test driven, fixed mindset outlooks of schooling is doing a remarkable job. To genuinely offer future-facing education in an English school is difficult. To do it well the school needs a brilliant Headteacher.

Read this book carefully. It is not a dip into book. The message needs to seep into the being of the reader. It is a step-by-step, build your own confidence through awareness, type book. It won't do the job for you but, if you read it well, think about the useful techniques and suggestions, and then put them into practice, you will be well on the way.

With experience, with a zest for the job of changing life chances, and with a sheer joy of learning in all its contexts, this book will help you to become a brilliant Headteacher.

Professor Mick Waters is president of the Curriculum Foundation, which seeks to promote a voice for the power and potential of the whole curriculum. Previously, he worked at the Qualifications and Curriculum Authority as Director of Curriculum. Before joining QCA, Mick was Chief Education Officer for the City of Manchester.

Introduction

The first people they kill are the teachers.

How do you start a book about what it takes to be a brilliant Headteacher? That question was the one that kept going over and over in my mind whilst planning this book. Quite an assumption to think that I am, or anyone is, brilliant. However I recognise there are many, many qualities that are needed to do this job well or even brilliantly. Teaching is the best job in the world and to be in charge of a school, to have the lives of hundreds of children pass through your hands, and having responsibility for the development of staff makes being a Headteacher the most exciting and best job in teaching. You can have a whole day planned out in front of you and you will sometimes get nothing done on the list – each day is unpredictable and that's one aspect of the job that makes it so interesting and challenging.

Whether you are a Head, a Governor, a member of staff, a parent or a child the key question to ask yourself is, what is it about my school that makes it unique? Is it something about the social and cultural mix? Is it the curriculum approach or the make-up of the staff and the governing body? As Heads we strive to create a school that suits its community, its staff, the physical environment it is set in and most of all the unique needs of those children who arrive each day to be educated under our care within those school grounds and beyond.

At the National College annual conference I went to one year I had the pleasure of listening to Kris Akabusi and Dame Kelly Holmes talk about success. Dame Kelly asked the audience what a Headteacher's 'Gold Medal' was. For her and Kris it was obvious – crossing the line first. For me the answer is simple, it is making a positive difference to children's lives. If just one former pupil comes up to you and tells you that if it was not for you they would not have achieved the success they had in their lives, then that is a gold medal. I believe we all came into teaching to make such a difference to children's lives. Kris and Dame Kelly could both point to a teacher that had made the difference to them. Dame Kelly, as soon as she arrived back in the UK after her double gold winning performance, phoned the teacher who had encouraged her to pursue a career in athletics, to thank her. As a Headteacher you influence not only the lives of the children in your care but the lives of the teachers and staff who care for those children on a day-to-day basis. On that basis you really do have to be brilliant at the job!

In this book I will explore in detail many of the things I have touched upon so far, but my inclination in this introduction is to identify the most important qualities for being a successful Headteacher. The word trust is one that I will explore later as it is central to successful headship and school leadership and is top of my list in what makes a successful Head and a successful school. Risk taking has to be high up there as well. From my love and interest in creativity you would be right to expect to find some creative thinking skills high up on my list of key qualities for successful headship.

As I passed through the ranks of the school management system in various schools without any career plan in mind, always insisting that I loved teaching so much that I would never become a Head, I gradually started to wish to see a school run in what I considered the best, most effective way. I watched some Heads I worked for do it brilliantly and others, from whom I learnt a great deal, do what I considered a less than effective job. This book started with acknowledgements and I must also thank those teachers and Headteachers who really did make a hash of things, for I learnt a great deal from them! I would not have had the success I have had if it was not for them and no doubt there are staff who have worked for me over the years who hopefully will become brilliant Headteachers on the back of some of the mistakes I have made.

No really successful school is about standardisation and uniformity. Inspectors will tell you that they get an immediate feel for the school they are inspecting and even what will be their overall judgement for a school after the first few minutes of entering it. Something hits you about the ethos, which has a unique feel about it. A good school has developed an ethos and a curriculum that suits its teachers, the school building and most importantly its children and community. Ultimately the creation of that ethos is down to the Head even if much of a school's success is down to what happens day to day within the four walls of a classroom and the interaction of the adults and the children in that room. A Head's influence can and must infiltrate those four walls as well.

Headship is about enabling others to be successful, be the best they can be, at every level of staffing, as well as the children and the extended school family of parents and carers. When leadership and headship become about yourself rather than those you are there to serve we start to see dictators and tyrants – but more of that later.

> headship is about enabling others to be successful

Often Heads will debate about who should be at the forefront of their thinking, the children or the staff. If you have not got happy staff how can you have happy children that are ready to learn? I, though, have always put the children as my ultimate priority. My current school's ethos, appearance and curriculum was inspired by the phrase, 'Do you know a place that makes you long for childhood?' If all our decisions, as Heads, are made on the basis that it benefits the children and/or the school then I believe that we are doing the job to the best of our ability and it often gives you the 'moral high ground' should there be a dispute. However inspiring a Head is, it is still vital to support and respect all staff and in the first place appoint the appropriate staff for the school. These are crucial ingredients for success as the school must belong to all its members. It is not 'my school' as Head, it has to be 'our school'.

CHAPTER 1

So what makes a successful Headteacher?

A successful school is like a living being; it seems as though it has its own life force which is immediately apparent as you open the door. Every Head rightly strives for their school to be the best it can be and there is no doubt that a school's success is determined by the quality of the Headteacher; how well we do our job is the key ingredient in determining the success of our school. In this first chapter we will explore the factors that make a school and its Head successful. What is the public perception of what a good Headteacher is? What are the qualities and attributes of the brilliant Headteacher? We will look at what skills you need and what it is that a Head does all day long whilst the teachers are hard at work in front of 30 willing young learners! This first chapter will consider whether a 'creative thinking, risk-taking Head' creates a successful school and how much a Head's personality, energy and optimism impacts on both personal successes and the success of the school. What are the key things to do and implement in a school so that we make a success of one of the most rewarding and challenging jobs there is?

The public perception of what makes a successful Headteacher

When the National College, in 2009, surveyed children about what sort of person makes a good Headteacher 60% of the children wanted someone who likes children. Some 50% wanted the

Head to have the ability to deal with difficult staff and children and 49% thought they needed to have good leadership skills. The children also wanted someone who had a kind personality but could be strict as well. Children thought that a Head needs determination and the ability to work with parents. The children surveyed felt that a Head's three most important jobs were; to ensure the teachers taught properly, to help everyone within the school to understand what the school is trying to do and to manage the school budget. How times have changed! This would not have been the case prior to the 1988 Education Act. Heads rarely watched teachers teaching and we did not even manage our own school budget.

In the same survey 64% of parents prioritised good leadership skills but only 31% felt it was a priority to like children! There was no reference to the Head being an outstanding or even good teacher in the classroom and this is perhaps indicative of not only how the job has changed but also how the public's perception of the job has changed. Parents and children seem to see the job more as a leadership role rather than the Head being a teacher. A Head of School rather than a Headteacher?

Personality characteristics of a Headteacher

Nowadays it seems that the kind of person you are, your personality and how confident you are as an individual are significant factors as to how you are perceived as a Headteacher.

The list of qualities for being a brilliant Head is endless. If like me you have an interest and passion for creativity and creative thinking then you may conclude that the greatest attributes a Head can have are those of a creative thinker. Alongside creative thinking surely have to be empathy and trust. The ability to put yourself in someone else's shoes, to share and understand another person's emotions and feelings is crucial in the headship role.

So if a brilliant Head is a creative Head then they need to be curious, courageous, determined, imaginative, collaborative and willing to take risks and make mistakes. Einstein famously said that he was not any more intelligent than anyone else: he just stuck at problems longer! It is a fascinating notion that the ability to take risks is a factor in being a brilliant Head. As Heads we can cultivate a culture whereby mistakes are seen as central to the learning process, for taking risks can often lead to significant success. A safety first approach can lead to mediocrity and stifle enterprise and creativity. When we trust someone and they trust us then decisions are made quickly and new leaders are developed.

The people person

Arguably a key factor in a Head's success is how emotionally intelligent they are, essentially how empathetic they are towards staff, children and the whole school community. Could a lot of it simply come down to how good a 'people person' we are? How often do we smile? How often do we make staff and children feel that they matter? Of course it is not as simple as that. As a Head we must use our time effectively, we need to be able to manage change successfully and we have to delegate responsibility in a structured and accountable way that impacts on the desired identified outcomes for our school.

Is, as many people suggest, the Head's job a lonely one? Most Heads would say that each day is far too busy for anyone ever to get lonely as the job has so much to do with people and interacting with those people – the staff, the children, the parents, the cooks, the cleaners, the office staff, the visitors and the contractors. The list goes on and has not even mentioned the Chair of Governors, the School Improvement Partner as well as the School Advisor and any Ofsted Inspectors that drop by from time to time. One thing is for sure, there is no time to feel alone and plenty of time to enjoy the company of colleagues, children and associates.

Is there a formula for being a brilliant Headteacher?

There are certain tasks performed by all successful Heads but it is important to remember that each school is different. As a Head we can have a very successful formula that works for the school we are currently in but move to another school and try the same things and we may fail. Many Heads rightly believe that it is important to role model the behaviours we wish to see throughout the school, the Head ultimately setting the whole climate for the school. Staff follow the model that is set for them by the Head and children follow the example that is set for them by the Head and the school staff. That is why when a Head changes in a school the school can go from a highly successful one to a failing school or the reverse. It is also why the same class of children can behave angelically for one teacher and demoniacally for another!

> it is important to role model the behaviours we wish to see

As Heads ourselves we must display bountiful energy and be full of enthusiasm for the job no matter what each day places in front of us; we must have an endless supply of optimism and hope for a better and more successful tomorrow. More importantly the school community must see the Head's optimism in order to replicate it themselves. As Heads we must be confident in what we are doing and what we believe in and stand for.

 **tip**

Not everyone will agree with decisions that are made but if they were made for the greater good, for the benefit of the school and the children in it and not out of self-interest or for personal ambition then you always have the moral high ground. You will never please all of the people all of the time and there are always those who are happier to be unhappy, and for them life is never full unless there is something to moan about. Part of a Head's job is of course to turn those people around and make the best of their hidden talents so that the school and children can benefit. It is too easy to avoid those staff and never go near their department or classroom – make the effort.

Sir Tim Brighouse suggests that a Head who has been in the same post for over five years is more likely to slip into complacency: should they therefore move on at that time? Remaining in post over a longer period of time can be one of the most significant challenges of headship. Sustaining improvement in one establishment for 10 years is very challenging, requires drive and motivation and is consequently very rewarding.

Education went through a time when the government was trying to urgently address the issue of what they perceived as failing schools by appointing a 'Super Head' to a failing school, often on only a 12-month brief, to sort the school out. Sometimes two such Heads may have been put into the school at inflated salary levels costing the Local Authority, who were under pressure to achieve rapid improvement, a great deal of money. In these cases there was often a significant turnover of staff and difficult children were permanently excluded in an effort to find the required short-term solution to the school's problems. In reality, if there is such a thing as a 'Super Head,' it is surely someone who goes into a school for the long haul, looking for long-term strategies that will benefit the whole school community, embedding practices and strategies that will develop learning and teaching to improve the life chances of the children in that school. This is not a one- or two-year project; real change will take up to four or five years to embed often requiring a paradigm shift in the school's ethos and educational philosophy.

Day-to-day working

So what do we as Heads do on a day-to-day basis? Firstly it will vary from individual to individual and from school to school. Some Heads are difficult to find and may have to be tracked down in the home corner in Reception, reading a story to some four year olds. Some Heads know the names of all the pre-school children who come into school with their parents and older brothers or sisters, because they are out on the playgrounds welcoming parents and children onto the school site and into the school building.

A Head's job involves a lot of reading and paperwork as well as checking the endless e-mails that queue up in the inbox for our attention each day. We as Heads must decide what balance suits us and our school's needs.

It is often very useful to get into school early and check e-mails, read the post and get on with paperwork. Staying late after school can be a time when some of the management issues are tackled. Of course there is your work–life balance to consider, but this can often be a misinterpreted term. Mrs Thatcher apparently liked to work for 15–20 hours a day and needed very little sleep and that was her ideal work–life balance. The reality is that if you are an ambitious person you are not going to get on in any walk of life without working hard and giving up a lot of your time. An NQT at our school was asked how his job was going in his first year in teaching. He replied that it wasn't a job, it was a way of life. For a committed person in a caring profession who wants to do their best for the children in their care it does become a way of life, especially for those who want to progress in the profession.

Teaching is a tremendously rewarding job but not a profession to join if you are looking for a 9–5 job. As practising Heads we know that this commitment is even further magnified in headship. As a result, as Sir Tim Brighouse describes, a common denominator with successful Heads is that they give up a lot of their evenings and weekends. He also points out that successful Heads know that during the day the whole school community is in school and that they need to be high profile, making the daily round of greeting staff, pupils and parents cheerfully as they welcome everyone into school. One Headteacher colleague said to me that his school was in his blood, it was part of him, a sentiment and feeling with which I totally concur.

brilliant tip

It is important, when you tour the school, to vary your route so that you get a chance to see different people at different times of the day – you then stand a better chance of seeing different parents each day of the week. Being available in this way demonstrates that you care and that you are interested in what is going on. This informal, unpredictable tour of the school also allows you to monitor what is going on around school and which staff are following school routines, like the warm welcoming of parents and children each day.

A high profile around school allows you to see if the children are on task and motivated to learn by what they are experiencing, effectively keeping your finger on the pulse of the school. During these tours it is critical that we appear happy, confident, positive and in control. It also makes you feel good as children, parents and staff will often greet you with a cheery smile and a warm welcome! However if there is a danger of emerging with a grumpy, unfriendly demeanour it is probably wisest to stay in your office! Our appearance as well as our mood can impact on the days of others, so we must make sure that we are focused on the children, staff and parents that surround us. If we fail to greet or smile they may wonder what they have done wrong! As

Heads we must strive for consistency of approach and this area is no exception.

 tip

> It is vital that as a Head (and for the school to be successful) you give everyone the impression that the positives, the good things, far outweigh the bad, negative issues. The school is going places and always on an upward trend, even when there are setbacks along the way.

The people person

A brilliant Headteacher in this day and age has to be a people person; you must be able to get on with both the Ofsted Inspector and the cleaner. I know the local authority groundsman by his first name and he knows me by mine; he supports Spurs, which I tolerate as a Manchester United supporter! I will get to know, by name, any builders who work on our site and the cook and cleaner are just as important as the teacher and the Office Manager if the school and children are to benefit and improve.

Schools can create a strong family feel; despite the size of our school the sense of unity of purpose is enhanced by the feeling that we are one large family … with 700 children to look after! However not everyone on the staff will always subscribe to the school ethos. Sadly some peoples lives are enriched by upsetting others and having the ability to find that one cloud in an otherwise totally blue sky, as a member of staff was once described to me. I have avidly read J.K. Rowling's Harry Potter books and it seems to me that staff fall broadly into two categories, with over 95% falling into the first. There are the Dumbledores who are positive and enthusiastic about the future, develop leaders, who embrace change and challenge and focus on what is best for the children in their care. Then there are the Dementors, thankfully a small minority of staff, who seem to want to suck the life out of everyone around them. As Head the latter cannot be ignored and part of the job is dealing with the more difficult staff or situations, so resilience, determination and perseverance, as well as honesty, with a healthy dose of empathy for others, are all important qualities of the brilliant Headteacher.

Good headship 'goes forward on a rising tide that will not always raise all the ships'. As Head you will not please all of the people, all of the time. Some Heads fail by trying to be Mr, Mrs or Ms Popular and will spend inordinate amounts of time trying to please everyone, but by making decisions that are for the greater good we gain others' respect if not always their agreement. One of the most important qualities, if not the most important of headship or leadership, is to make sure that in your decisions you put aside your own needs and prioritise the needs of others. When, as a Head, the needs of humanity come first you begin to realise the importance and significance of headship and how important it is to become brilliant at it. By leading the educators and those being educated we have an influence in a small way, individually, but as a collective profession in a huge way on the world's future.

> you will not please all of the people, all of the time

brilliant example

I was once told that when rebels invade a village or town in some of the war-torn regions of the world, the first people they kill are the teachers! One example of influence.

Super Heads?

We would all agree that a Head cannot be some sort of super-human being. We are human, but equally, there is no denying that expectations of a Head are high from every area of society. As Heads we will not have the answer to everything: however we may know someone who does have the answer or we can often find out and solve the challenge with the help of others. It may be that as Heads we ask more questions than anyone else! It is also important that we do not feel that we must give an answer there and then; it is more important that we give the most helpful response that we can and that may mean researching and reflecting on it. If we try to be the font of all knowledge then we will have disempowered others and find that our job quickly becomes unmanageable. Not every question or issue that we are asked will be of interest to us, but it may well be that for the person asking the question the success of their day may hang upon our response. As a Head we must accept that we have to be interested in everything, and on every occasion with each person who needs our support or advice, show that interest overtly. We all know that the 'personal touch' makes a big difference and we must strive consistently to demonstrate such an interest in all individuals. It is important to ensure that staff know how grateful we are when they do something well or find the answer to an issue the school is trying to address. As Sir Tim Brighouse says, 'the congratulatory or thankful word in the corridor or in a staff or school newsletter again makes such a difference to the overall success of the school'. Oil all the smaller cogs on a regular basis and the efficiency of the whole school's engine will benefit.

brilliant dos and don'ts

Do

- ✔ Do take inspiration from every leader for whom you work.
- ✔ Do ensure you create a unique school ethos.
- ✔ Do base all your decisions on the needs of others, specifically the children in your school.

Don't

✗ Don't visualise 'My School', ensure it will be 'Our School'.

✗ Don't neglect development of your interpersonal skills.

Head of School or Headteacher?

Most Heads will agree that one of the challenges of Headship is to keep up to date with current initiatives and changes in government policies, Ofsted inspection practices and the sheer amount of reading associated with this. It is important to be ahead of staff in these areas, so that we are highlighting for them what the future holds and so helping them and the school to be successful.

More than ever before staff want a Head to be good at the job of headship and not necessarily a wonderful classroom practitioner. In the past there was always a strong argument that Heads must be good classroom practitioners but the whole educational landscape has changed in recent years – there are many more distinctive layers of management, leadership and responsibility and a Head's job is very different and distinctive compared to 20 years ago. In addition to this if we are not in a classroom day to day we quickly become de-skilled as practitioners, but we do become up-skilled in what we have to do as Head. Most of us would agree that Ofsted Inspectors, like Heads, need to have been practising teachers but it is just as impractical for them to keep returning to the classroom as, like Heads, they become very good at the job they are doing. An Inspector, like a Head, will have seen so many lessons that they are very skilled at accurately spotting an outstanding, good, satisfactory or inadequate lesson.

> a Head's job is very different and distinctive compared to 20 years ago

So how can we as Heads keep up this pace? Early mornings, late evenings, working at home both at the weekends and during the evenings as well as giving up time to the school during holidays! It comes down to finding a work–life balance that suits you as an individual. It is not something that you can prescribe or make recommendations about. As Heads we love the job of Headship and are willing to give up a lot of time to school if it means that the school and the pupils are going to benefit. There are times when family life and the needs of family members must come first, but equally there are times and circumstances when the job must come first.

brilliant recap

As Heads we are responsible to the whole school community and our job is basically to do all we can to support it. Getting our work–life balance appropriate is vital, as is remembering that the job is not just about ourselves and our career. We are there to serve the whole school community and support them. We must not underestimate the fact that the success of the school hinges on us as Heads, more than any other individual. Successes are of course down to others and we take responsibility for failures but at the same time we are eternal optimists and we are running the best school in the land!

CHAPTER 2

Becoming a Headteacher

This chapter will take us back to the first steps we take when wanting to be a Head but with a modern day slant. It focuses on how to become a Headteacher and the challenges and requirements of the NPQH (National Professional Qualification for Headship) process. First we look at the implications of going for headship and then focus on each of the standards and give suggestions as to how to meet them.

There are six standards and between them they cover all the main skills and qualities that are needed to be a Head and provide the applicant with a tailor-made personalised route to starting headship as well equipped as they can be without actually doing the job. As Heads we also need to know the standards well so that we can support and assess a Deputy Head who aspires to pass the NPQH standards. The NPQH website and the National Standards for Headteachers guide you through the process and have been used to support the information in this chapter and ensure accuracy.

Before you can be appointed as a Headteacher you have to gain the NPQH. As the NPQH website describes:

it is a personalised programme based on each individual's development needs. Once on the NPQH programme you can get access to a wide range of support including national learning materials, placements in other schools, coaching from an identified colleague as well as online resources and local leadership development activities. On entering the NPQH programme you must be judged to be ready for Headship within the next 12–18 months with the full support of your Headteacher or line manager. To apply you have to demonstrate your effectiveness in line with the National Standards for Headteachers via a very detailed and demanding process of self and peer assessment that, if successful, culminates in a two day intensive National College assessment. If deemed to be successful you become a Trainee Headteacher. A coach is available to work with you as you address your agreed personal areas for development. This development phase takes between 4 to 12 months depending upon how close the candidate is to headship and how quickly they address their identified development areas.

The NPQH is based around six areas of assessment that I will analyse in turn, describing the requirements within each to pass the NPQH assessment. In applying for NPQH you will need the full support of your Headteacher, who is willing to allow you to experience all facets of their role including, most importantly, decision making.

↗ brilliant case study

I was inspired to apply for NPQH in May 2009 after settling successfully into a senior leadership role as a non-teaching Deputy Head. At Local Authority meetings succession planning was always high on the agenda and I'd listened to many different speakers encouraging us (a group of Deputy Heads) to consider applying for the new NPQH. I submitted my application, swiftly completed over half term, with the full support of my Headteacher. With hindsight I think everyone I'd spoken to locally about applying was somewhat under-informed of how NPQH had changed, particularly in terms of the rigour applied through the application process.

Great disappointment struck in the Summer of 2009 when I learned my written application had not been successful but the feedback sent by the National College for Leadership of Schools and Children's Services was detailed and very useful. I set about ensuring that opportunities to collect evidence in the relevant areas were in place for the new academic year. Second time around I took a great deal more care over collecting and collating evidence referring constantly to the National Standards for Headteachers and my initial application feedback. I spoke with my Headteacher during our performance management process and secured an internship at a contrasting school during which time I spoke at length with that Headteacher about my application. These reflective, professional dialogues were very useful in clarifying my thoughts. Further reassurance arrived when I took up the offer of a telephone conversation with a representative from NCSL regarding application. Discussing my application with an impartial, well-informed advisor was invaluable and an activity I would recommend to anyone preparing to apply for NPQH.

Better preparation second time around proved to be successful and I was delighted to hear that my application had secured me a place at an NPQH two-day development event. There was preparation to be done by way of a 360° diagnostic exercise and initial work on a Personal Development Record (PDR) both based closely on the Headteacher Standards. The feedback that I received from colleagues through the 360° diagnostic was thought-provoking and I found discussion of the outcomes with my Headteacher both challenging and supportive in equal measure. The realisation that as a leader my intentions are not always manifested in perceptions of my behaviour as I would hope was one of the pivotal moments in my journey towards headship. I believe everyone in the teaching profession should have the opportunity to receive formal feedback from those with whom they work in this way.

The NPQH two-day development event ranks amongst the most memorable and challenging events of my life due to the pace, depth and rigour of the assessed activities as well as the degree of self-reflection involved. Whilst the process was physically, emotionally and mentally exhausting I can also state that it left me in no doubt about my strengths as a leader as well as my key areas for development. The colleagues with whom I shared this experience all agree it left us sharing a special bond and those of us who are now officially Trainee Headteachers intend to continue to support each other as an NPQH Peer Learning Group. The assessors who led us through ▶

the two days were fair, professional and supportive; I was reassured during my detailed personal feedback at the end of the process that they had obtained an accurate picture of me as a leader, and it was very rewarding to be told immediately that I had been successful.

The most recent stage of my NPQH journey has been attending a regional NPQH introductory day where the learning process was explained fully. As a group of 40 Trainee Headteachers we were taken through a wealth of opportunities available to us at rapid pace through a packed day into which the facilitators somehow also managed to schedule regular personal reflection and peer support. The day was motivating for me with its over-riding message that NPQH is highly personalised training; the model of devising my own action plan and judging when I am ready to graduate with the support of a coach rather than a mentor seems in itself to be excellent preparation for the role of headship!

From the moment I decided I would like to be a Headteacher through the disappointments and trials of applying for NPQH (which should not be under-estimated!) I have learnt a huge amount about myself as a leader but also as a person. I look forward to continuing my learning journey and to the opportunity to be a Headteacher who can inspire adults and children alike.

Standard 1: Shaping the future

Critical to the role of headship is working with the governing body and others to create a shared vision and strategic plan which inspires and motivates pupils, staff and all other members of the school community. This vision should express core educational values and moral purpose and be inclusive of stakeholders' values and beliefs. The strategic planning process is critical to sustaining school improvement and ensuring that the school moves forward for the benefit of its pupils.

(National Standards for Headteachers, DfES2004: 6)

This is a very interesting area as it is asking the aspiring Head to look at how they have created a shared vision for the school that inspires and motivates the school community. The school's vision is often associated primarily with the incumbent Headteacher; one of the recognised traits of a successful school is that the Head has a very clear vision for the future. Providing evidence of your impact in this area can therefore be quite challenging as in most established schools there is a shared vision that has already been created by the school, its staff, pupils, parents and governors.

brilliant tips

To address this part of 'Shaping the future':

- Get involved with the governing body.
- Get to know the community by meeting local groups and becoming involved with local initiatives.
- Form relationships with Governors, staff, parents and the local community.
- Get to know the thoughts, wishes and dreams of the whole community.
- Make decisions based on what the school community wants and not on what you may think they want.

Within the 'established school' there may be things you can do to make an impact on the school's vision. Focus on what the school is doing or needs to be improved upon and you may find areas where you could have a valuable input, for example developing provision for Special Needs or Gifted and Talented children.

A school's vision is rooted in raising standards so look for areas of development that you can affect, embedding a culture of high expectations and excellence, whilst leading by example. A school's vision will be based upon doing the best for all children regardless of their social or cultural background. Is there an opportunity to develop links with outside agencies? Does the school need to set up a support system for children with behavioural or emotional needs? The school may also need its curriculum developing to become more creative or innovative, or to embrace new technologies, in its aim to achieve excellence. It would be unusual for there to be no areas for development that would directly impact on issues that help 'shape the future' of the school.

 **brilliant** recap

A visionary leader communicates a compelling view of the future to all staff. Such a leader acts according to personal principles and values, embraces change, will deliver improved results, values others and makes colleagues feel more confident in their abilities.

Standard 2: Leading learning and teaching

Headteachers have a central responsibility for raising the quality of teaching and learning and for pupils' achievement. This implies setting high expectations and monitoring and evaluating the effectiveness of learning outcomes. A successful learning culture will enable pupils to become effective, enthusiastic, independent learners, committed to life-long learning.

(National Standards for Headteachers, DfES2004: 7)

To be successful in this area you need a good working knowledge of assessment and tracking procedures and the ability to hold staff accountable for pupils' progress and standards. A good understanding of pupil progress data and its analysis is essential. In terms of headship the key thing is to have a system

> a good understanding of pupil progress data and its analysis is essential

whereby you can hold all staff accountable for the progress of every child in their care. In preparing for NPQH application you need to lead and coordinate the analysis and accountability procedures of the school's assessment arrangements.

brilliant tips

There are always new initiatives on the horizon, for change is the one constant thing in education, and so there will always be an opportunity to introduce something new into a school for those who are brave and enthused enough to make a difference.

● Seek to introduce a new initiative into your school's assessment approach.

● Try to make an impact on issues like attendance and punctuality as well as on standards and achievement in learning.

● Endeavour to lead the development of extended services, particularly in the fields of behaviour management, parent support and emotional/social support.

To meet the requirements of this standard you need to challenge underperformance in the school in whatever form it may appear.

Standard 3: Developing self and working with others

Effective relationships and communication are important in headship as Headteachers work with and through others. Effective Headteachers manage themselves and their relationships well. Headship is about building a professional learning community which enables others to achieve. Through performance management and effective continuing professional development practice, the Headteacher supports all staff to achieve high standards. To equip themselves with the capacity to deal with the complexity of the role and the range of leadership skills and actions required of them, Headteachers should be committed to their own continuing professional development.

(National Standards for Headteachers, DfES/0083/2004: 8)

The days of the Headteacher as the oracle, the answer to everything, are long gone. Nowadays the key to success lies in the effectiveness of the team that runs the school and so quality of relationships and communication are key factors. Distributed leadership models that engage all staff in decision making at an appropriate level include plenty of opportunities for aspiring Heads to work effectively with others as well as developing themselves as leaders. High up on any school's agenda must be succession planning and so part of this standard will be met by developing other staff into more senior roles in school through in-service training, professional development and the performance management cycle.

brilliant example

Many schools have moved away from employing supply teachers who more often than not were unable to manage the children's learning. Schools have now trained and continue to train a number of very talented support staff as Higher Level Teaching Assistants (HLTAs) or Cover Supervisors who have to meet standards, assessed by an external moderator, which for HLTAs are very similar to those for Newly Qualified Teachers (NQTs).

Developing support staff by providing in-house training or brokering courses with the Local Authority on their behalf would be valid evidence in this area.

One of the key factors for this standard is how well the candidate works with others and therefore peer assessment by colleagues is a crucial factor. It is very easy when you are focused on meeting the NPQH standards to see it as a tick list of standards but you must ensure this is not the impression that colleagues have of your motivation. It is here that the maxim 'when there are successes it is down to others and when there are failures it is down to the leader of the initiative' comes into play. If you have apportioned credit to others with initiatives that you have led, then it will generally be seen by others that you work well with colleagues. However for the purposes of NPQH application you are required to cite exclusively your own personal impact on the school. Of course a balance is needed as you do not want to be seen as relying on others but equally you need to be seen as a team player and able to work with others. A collaborative leader will consult and take on board the ideas of others but is strong enough to make the final decision even when it is a contentious and difficult one.

To achieve this standard you must demonstrate that you can build a successful collaborative learning community where you are seen as someone who can support and develop others and their ideas. A credible leader focuses on professional development and learning, coaches and helps others to improve through collaborative strategies, and guards against their own self-interest being the key motivation for action. You need to be perceived as the democratic leader, not an autocratic one, but capable of making difficult decisions or handling difficult situations decisively when necessary.

> a credible leader focuses on professional development and learning

brilliant tips

- Consult with others, take their ideas on board, feed back developments and key decisions decisively.

- Treat people fairly, equitably, with dignity and respect so that a positive school culture is maintained.
- Be particularly pro-active when managing conflict.
- Ensure that you acknowledge the responsibilities of others and celebrate the achievements of individuals and teams.
- Be acutely aware of your impact on the work–life balance of others.

A great deal of self-development can be achieved by simply following the requirements of the NPQH standards and making achieving those standards an integral part of your performance management cycle. The process itself is designed to develop the candidate and so by working towards achieving the standards you will be developing yourself professionally. NPQH encourages self-assessment and assessment by others at all steps providing a more objective view of yourself upon which you can act.

As the NPQH website describes, each Trainee Headteacher is given a Personal Development Record (PDR):

a working document for identifying strengths and development needs documenting activities undertaken and reflecting on progress towards graduation. It provides you with a personal pathway of development priorities and allows you to reflect on your learning and progress based on all of your pre-assessment diagnostic tools, including the 360° diagnostic, a confidential, on-line assessment of your capabilities completed anonymously by colleagues which is externally analysed.

(www.nationalcollege.org.uk)

At the two-day assessment and development event you can share your PDR with an assessor. Within the PDR you identify strengths and development areas and provide evidence to support your findings. The two-day assessment is very intense and should you be assessed as not being ready to progress further towards graduation then the evidence gathered and the PDR will be invaluable when you re-apply. The PDR asks you to identify strengths, development areas and actions, and to reflect on and summarise your consequent learning; it is a personal journey tailor made to your own needs.

Standard 4: Managing the organisation

Headteachers need to provide effective organisation and management of the school and seek ways of improving organisational structures and functions based on rigorous self-evaluation. Headteachers should ensure that the school and the people and the resources within it are organised and managed to provide an efficient, effective and safe learning environment. These management responsibilities imply the re-examination of the roles and responsibilities of those adults working in the school to build capacity across the workforce and ensure resources are deployed to achieve value for money. Headteachers should also seek to build successful organisations through effective collaborations with others.

(National Standards for Headteachers, DfES/0083/2004: 9)

This area asks you to develop plans based on robust evidence demonstrating ability for school improvement planning. You must demonstrate that you are supportive to staff by showing your awareness that they need to maintain a work–life balance. This standard asks the candidate to show that they are aware of the need for an effective distributed leadership model that encourages leadership and responsibility amongst others. It expands into your ability to work collaboratively with others beyond your own school, with other schools and agencies. Within this area of headship it is important to show that as a leader you can go straight to the heart of an issue and think and act clearly and decisively, demonstrating good judgement. The areas in which you may not have had much experience, with respect to school management, are health and safety, finance, personnel, and site and buildings maintenance, as Heads will, out of necessity, automatically take the lead in these areas. You can get involved in Governor's Committees to engage in the strategic decision making with respect to the management of the school. Attending such strategic thinking groups will give you the opportunity to look at evaluating the impact of managing the school's total resources, in the widest sense, so that you can get an idea of whether the school is providing good value for money in terms of improving the quality of education for all children.

brilliant example

There are comparative websites that are very useful to use in terms of benchmarking your budget with those from other schools. Such sites allow you to compare your school to other schools in terms of what percentage of your budget you spend on each area. These sites allow you to compare yourself with similar schools as well. For example those with comparable numbers, ethnicity, socio-economics, free school meals or age of school. They will also allow you to quarry even deeper and compare what sums are spent on Special Educational Needs (SEN) or Gifted and Talented (G&T) children compared to other schools. One such site, Financial Benchmarking for Schools describes itself as follows:

This site enables you to prepare charts that compare your school's income and expenditure profile with that of similar schools. The web site now includes information for all maintained schools in England through Consistent Financial Reporting. Any school, LA or guest can use this site and select its own group of similar schools, using a range of factors such as size, type, percentage with special needs and so on.

(https://sfb.teachernet.gov.uk)

To meet this standard you also need to demonstrate capability in recruiting, line managing, developing staff and developing school policies. Particularly important are policies that are legally required to be in place, such as employment, redundancy, complaints, confidentiality and whistle-blowing. Schools will subscribe to an independent personnel advisory company or to Local Authority-based advice where you can get legally correct policies that can then be personalised to your own school and adopted by the Governors.

The whole area of risk assessment is very important; you need experience of completing risk assessments for school trips and other school events, the school grounds, the classrooms and other areas of school. All such assessments and policies need to be up to date, part of a review cycle and accessible to staff.

The area of safeguarding is critical as Ofsted inspections now prioritise it. Issues such as the safety of the school grounds, CRB checks and safer recruitment are included. In this highly accountable field you need the support of professional advice, someone to contact and check your every step when it comes to legalities in what can be the more challenging aspects of headship. For the prospective Head this is an area of which you must be fully aware.

Standard 5: Securing accountability

With values at the heart of their leadership, Headteachers have a responsibility to the whole school community. In carrying out this responsibility, Headteachers are accountable to a wide range of groups, particularly pupils, parents, carers, Governors and the LEA [Local Education Authority]. They are accountable for ensuring that pupils enjoy and benefit from a high quality education, for promoting collective responsibility within the whole school community and for contributing to the education service more widely. Headteachers are legally and contractually accountable to the governing body for the school, its environment and its work.

(National Standards for Headteachers, DfES/0083/2004: 10)

Schools are measured on results; their ability to raise standards and improve achievement. This area of securing accountability focuses on the performance of the school according to how Ofsted and external inspections measure it. It is no good if a football team promotes itself on the quality of its ground, the design of its football kit or the quality of its catering if it is losing matches! In school, it may be very frustrating that inspections do not recognise much of the outstanding work we do as schools but if they are measuring very specific areas upon which to form their judgements, then we need to ensure we are performing well in those areas. To achieve high standards means getting all those other factors in place like good behaviour, an engaging and stimulating learning environment, a unique school ethos, a wide range of extra-curricular activities, a truly broad and balanced curriculum and of course a smart school uniform, healthy food and a good quality football pitch!

Every school needs a robust tracking system that analyses and creates targets holding all staff accountable for delivering agreed results. Managing and coordinating such a system is key to meeting this standard. Analysis of data combined with the findings of lesson observations, pupil interviews and book scrutinies should enable leaders to recognise both achievement and underperformance in all areas of school. Key to success for the school as well as providing evidence for this standard is to ensure staff, year groups and departments are held clearly accountable based upon honest and open feedback that recognises, through this constructive feedback, areas of strength and development. Through both this form of feedback as well as Performance Management (PM) targets (PM cannot cover all areas of the curriculum or all your areas of responsibility), staff must be made aware of what both their short- and long-term targets are and how these fit into the bigger school picture for whole school improvement. However you look at it, this is a key area of headship to master as it concentrates on the areas that are so often the focus of external inspections and judgements.

every school needs a robust tracking system

brilliant tips

- Avoid the temptation of micro-management focusing on the areas that need improving to the detriment of staff involvement and ownership in the process, failing to recognise and celebrate successes.

- Ensure you are involved in the feedback of results/progress with the School Improvement Partner, the Local Authority, the Governors and of course Ofsted when any of them appear on the school doorstep. Part of this process would be to get involved in the writing of the school's Self-Evaluation Form (SEF) as this is the main format for summarising a school's targets, actions and impact.

Standard 6: Strengthening community through collaboration

Schools exist in a distinctive social context, which has a direct impact on what happens inside the school. School leadership should commit to engaging with the internal and external community to ensure equity and entitlement. Headteachers should collaborate with other schools in order to share expertise and bring positive benefits to their own and other schools. They should work collaboratively at both strategic and operational levels with parents and carers and across multiple agencies for the well-being of all children. Headteachers share responsibility for leadership of the wider educational system and should be aware that school improvement and community development are interdependent.

As the NPQH website states:

this standard is all about strengthening the school's work with the whole school community in its widest sense, it is about your ability to work with other professions, with families and the local community, with organisations and agencies that impact on and support the school as well as understanding and dealing with how the dynamics of such a diverse range of groups vary from one to another. An emphasis is placed upon your ability to articulate and embed in a school the principles of the Every Child Matters agenda. [now called 'Helping Children to Achieve More']

(National Standards for Headteachers, DfES/0083/2004: 11)

Headship, more than almost any other job in any other profession, entails working with an incredibly diverse range of people from all walks of life. In a school that is both socially and culturally diverse, as so many are nowadays, the parent population alone presents you with a wide range of individual needs and expectations.

Success in this area of headship necessitates having respect and sometimes tolerance for all professionals with whom you work. The overriding consideration is the greater good of the school, so it is crucial to work with enthusiasm and interest with all community partners. It is important to value all input from all these partners as this will contribute to further strengthening and supporting the school community. In dealing with all the professionals and non-professionals that engage with a school the key to success is not so much the ability to contribute and help but to be able to listen and act upon the advice of others. Empathetic and

> it is crucial to work with enthusiasm and interest with all community partners

understanding leaders who see themselves as life-long learners will be in a better position to strengthen the school community as they will be more likely to be seen as people that others can turn to in times of need.

Consider involvement in the SEN work of the school, Child Protection and Looked After Children issues to engage with a wide range of external agencies. Most schools organise meetings with parents when their child's attendance drops below a certain level and this is a strategy that can actually strengthen relationships with parents as both parties get to know each other better and empathise with each other's situations.

Schools are often part of a local network of schools and this is an opportunity to engage with other school leaders and professional colleagues that can also be a catalyst for local in-service training. Such groups are worth getting actively involved with as they can further strengthen the wider school community to the benefit of both staff and children. The Extended Schools and Children's Centre agendas have created further opportunities for collaboration with external agencies and other schools so should be embraced if the opportunity arises.

The Children's Act of 2004 introduced one of the best agendas, in my opinion, to be produced by government: Every Child Matters (ECM). To meet this final standard you must look at the six areas of ECM – Being Healthy, Staying Safe, Enjoying and Achieving, Making a Positive Contribution and Achieving Economic Well-being – and find areas to develop within your school. Each area of ECM highlights important areas for schools to address. These are reminiscent of Maslow's hierarchy of needs, in which he emphasised the needs and rights of people and the community to be safe, enjoy loving relationships, have somewhere to sleep and something to eat and drink as well as enjoying the respect from and of others without prejudice. It is important to articulate your belief in the principles and areas of

Every Child Matters and demonstrate how you have embedded practices that support ECM in your school.

brilliant recap

Headship is a very rewarding job but it is a step that must not be taken lightly, which is why the NPQH process must be welcomed as it so comprehensively prepares someone for headship. Each of the standards combined, as the NPQH website describes, 'cover all the areas of Headship and provide the applicant with an excellent pathway of personalised development that enhances that individual's professional development whether or not they make it to successful graduation at the end of the process.' It gives each applicant the opportunity to have a comprehensive insight into the job of headship and be certain that it is the route they want to pursue. Once in post a new Head can expect support from fellow Headteachers, the school Governors and the Local Authority. The level of this support may vary from one Local Authority to another.

CHAPTER 3

Leading a school

This chapter will look at what qualities are needed to be an effective leader. But what do we mean by effective leadership? BNET, the business directory, defines leadership as,

the capacity to establish direction and to influence and align others toward a common goal, motivating and committing them to action and making them responsible for their performance.

It is interesting that a business definition of leadership is applicable to school leadership. As leaders we must have the ability to influence people to move in a certain pre-determined direction to achieve the school's agreed goals, but if we allow leadership to become about ourselves rather than the needs of the school community we will fail as leaders. School leadership is not about what the Headteacher wants, even though we will often make the final decisions, but rather ensuring the school community shares ownership of the school's ambitions. As Heads we must influence the school community to support what we, the leading professionals, set out as the school's vision for future success. A good leader motivates staff and effectively deploys human and material resources to support the objectives they wish to achieve. This chapter will look at what constitutes good leadership, the importance of trust in an organisation and the need for effective leaders to facilitate an ethos of leadership at all levels and so actively encourage succession planning.

 **tip**

A leader's human qualities, together with their ability to complete assigned tasks, inform judgement of their leadership effectiveness.

Raising standards and improving lives

Christine Gilbert, the government's Chief Inspector of Schools in 2009, described a Headteacher's core purpose as, 'raising standards and improving lives'. She quite rightly pointed out the impact a good Headteacher has on a school and described the job as a balancing act but stated that all good Heads have one thing in common: a strong sense of purpose.

At the 2009 National College conference the theme was 'the moral imperative' as the main driving force behind a Head's motivation. Christine Gilbert summarised that good Heads 'ensure that the school is a calm and positive place, where lessons are consistently well taught and learning is the top priority'. She went on to say that Heads 'need courage, determination and resilience if they are to avoid being discouraged or deflected. They must also be skilled, persuasive and sensitive communicators. While this may be important for all leaders, few in any other field have to communicate with such a wide range of different groups.'

Headship is a challenging but rewarding job that Christine Gilbert clearly understands well. Headship must not be entered into lightly; the weight of responsibility is the most significant factor that becomes evident once you are in post and the NPQH qualification is an appropriately thorough preparation.

Christine Gilbert also described good Heads as 'being realistic and level-headed. They diagnose their schools' strengths and weaknesses wisely and dispassionately'. Heads need all the skills she lists because although the majority of the job is rewarding and stimulating Heads are also very likely to have to address difficult situations in the knowledge that they are ultimately accountable: accusations against staff – true and false – redundancy procedures, dealing with acts of unprofessional conduct, capability processes with underperforming staff or even accusations against oneself.

brilliant case study

A Deputy Head was responsible for the school for a day while the Headteacher led an overseas visit. The Deputy had released herself to be available most of the time and this proved to be very prudent. The following list of unforeseen events is genuinely what took place that day: a distraught parent arrived with serious concerns about his children's safety with their step-father, the fire alarm went off, the local PCSO (Police Constable Supporting Officer) arrived to interview two children about vandalism, a child protection concern was logged about possible physical abuse of a four-year-old whose parents spoke no English, a drunk intruder presented violently on school premises five minutes before the children were due to go home and the Local Authority Designated Officer called regarding a serious allegation against a member of staff. All of the issues were dealt with, and the Deputy learnt a valuable accountability lesson about headship!

The core purpose of the job

The 1998 Teacher Training Agency National Standards for Headteachers definition of the 'Core purpose of the Headteacher', describes the purpose of Headship as ensuring 'high quality education for all their pupils and improved standards of learning and achievement'.

It goes on say:

The Headteacher is the leading professional in the school. Working with the governing body, the Headteacher provides vision, leadership and direction for the school and ensures that it is managed and organised to meet its aims and targets. With the governing body, the Headteacher is responsible for the continuous improvement in the quality of education; for raising standards; for ensuring quality of opportunity for all; for the development of policies and practices; and for ensuring that resources are efficiently and effectively used to achieve the school's aims and objectives. The Headteacher also secures the commitment of the wider community to the school, by developing and maintaining effective networks with, for example, other local schools, the Local Authority, higher education institutions, employers, careers services and others. The Headteacher is responsible for creating a productive, disciplined learning environment and for the day-to-day management, organisation and administration of the school, and is accountable to the governing body.

Succession planning

There is a constantly evolving need for school leaders to make succession planning one of the key issues that schools need to seriously address. Headship has dramatically changed over the past 20 years and for the first time in education history there is now the real possibility of progressing from Teaching Assistant to Headteacher.

It is worth addressing the premise that all children and adults are leaders or potential leaders – a leader in every seat – and it is particularly important for all members of staff to be leaders and to develop the qualities of good leadership. A Head's responsibility is to encourage and foster leadership in others; opportunities must be given within the existing decision-making structure of the

> all children and adults are leaders or potential leaders

school for all staff to feel safe to offer ideas, implement change and in doing so feel safe to fail and learn from their mistakes because appropriate support and monitoring systems are in place.

The *Times Educational Supplement* quoted Sue Hoyle, director of the Clore Leadership Programme, when she highlights ten qualities that make a good leader:

1. A passion for your job so that you enthuse and inspire those around you.

2. Proven achievement in translating vision into action.

3. A self-awareness that allows you to recognise both your strengths and your weaknesses.

4. Motivation that gives you a strong sense of purpose.

5. An effective communicator in writing, orally, in the use of technology, as a presenter and as a negotiator whilst always being sensitive to the interests of others.

6. An enquiring mind that has the capacity to reflect and learn.

7. Sound judgement that allows you to analyse complex information, assess risk and make appropriate choices and decisions.

8. A team player who has the ability to motivate and develop others whilst setting high standards and expectations of yourself and others.

9. Flexibility that enables you to think laterally and creatively.

10. Integrity so that you demonstrate honesty, authenticity, humility and openness.

When there is an opportunity for leadership tasks or roles to be taken on then staff should feel confident to assume more responsibility and they would not go too far wrong by considering and following Sue Hoyle's ten qualities of leadership. Leaders must prepare the ground for those to come and ensure staff are aware of the qualities that make a good leader.

What to look for in a potential leader:

- Leaders must always want to change the world for the better.
- Leaders work with a moral purpose putting aside their personal needs.
- Leaders do the right thing for the greater good.

What is a leader?

At the National College annual conferences I have made notes and listened to a wide range of speakers talking about the factors that make a successful leader. Here are some of the sound bites that have resonated with me:

- 'Leaders lead by example and great leaders grow leaders whereas tyrants keep people down.'
- 'Some people get to a certain position of power and change from a wonderful warrior into a bloody tyrant and from a great teacher to a bullying leader.'
- 'A leader is a dealer in hope.'
- 'If you are not willing to put your head above the parapet you will never be a successful leader.'
- 'Some leaders get obsessed with pleasing everyone and keeping everyone happy; they lose the respect of others.'
- 'Good leadership is about a rising tide that does not lift all the boats.'
- 'Leadership must be based on a deep inner core of values and beliefs that benefit the vast majority of the community. Good leaders serve their whole community.'
- 'There will be times when you need to be a warrior but some get addicted to the buzz of crisis and being in the

"driving position" and they cannot get out of it and it becomes dangerous and counter-productive; this leads to failure, not success.'

Figure 3.1 shows a grid used by Richard Olivier to very successfully summarise different types of leaders. I have found it to be a useful tool for self- and peer evaluation.

Trust and alignment

Leadership qualities are wide ranging and one of the biggest changes over the past 30 years is that leadership styles in education have changed significantly. There were undoubtedly schools years ago that controlled children through fear culminating in the use of corporal punishment, where leadership

Figure 3.1 Four different types of leader

(*source*: Richard Olivier, National College Conference, 2008) was all-powerful and as a result we sometimes saw tyrants and dictatorial leaders. In the past there were some Heads that ruled through fear and would divide staff in an attempt to rule effectively. Traditionally everyone turned to the Head as the person who made all the decisions and had all the answers: there was little evidence of delegation or distributed leadership strategies. That old style of leadership has gradually disappeared so that it now hardly exists. Since those days research has taken place examining effective leadership qualities and successful leaders nowadays trust and build trust through credibility, positive behaviour and confidence.

Trust

At the 2008 annual National College Conference for Heads the Canadian, Stephen Covey, talked about the 13 behaviours of high trust leaders: the ability to talk straight, demonstrate respect, create transparency, right wrongs, show loyalty, deliver results, get better, confront reality, clarify expectations, practise accountability, listen first, keep commitments and extend trust.

Stephen Covey's key quality of leadership is trust. Trust takes a long time to embed in a school but it is in many ways the most important factor to cultivate and achieve and once established it must be maintained as it takes even longer to regain. As Covey describes, when there is trust decisions are made quickly, people are on the same wavelength, you are supportive of each other, you enjoy open communication with no misunderstandings, there is a pleasant relaxed atmosphere and mistakes are understood. People who enjoy trust are positively energised by each other and find joy in working together. One person in an organisation, especially in a senior position, that cannot be trusted or does not trust others can change the ethos of trust and so make our schools less effective. If there is trust in an organisation, in a school, positive changes can occur and spread across the whole organisation to staff, children and parents. Covey's research suggests that test scores can triple, as well as pupils' behaviour and attitudes improving!

Stephen Covey talks about the importance and significance of trust in an organisation. Trust is hard to achieve, especially for the new Head. Forming relationships and establishing yourself as a Head in a school brings the challenge of earning the respect and trust of all the stakeholders, which can take time. Covey goes on to describe how trust has a ripple effect, meaning that appointments to our schools are vitally important and great care must be taken when appointing staff to trust that the new recruit will adhere to the school ethos. As Heads we must seek to appoint staff who articulate a genuine interest in the school, who are full of energy and drive, and who submit a personalised job application containing convincing reasons for why they want to work particularly at the school to which they are applying. Having appointed staff we will observe them carefully to judge not only their effectiveness but also how trustworthy they are; the more trustworthy someone is the more likely we are to promote them, and the more quickly we will support their decisions in important matters.

Covey describes how when trust does not exist in an establishment then staff tend towards suspicion delaying decisions by searching for ulterior motives. A lack of trust will often result in cautious, guarded or even defensive decision making with wide-ranging manifestations but where there is trust, decision-making processes run smoothly and efficiently saving both money and time.

Trust is a key factor in success and the good news according to MORI is that teachers (as well as doctors) are the most trusted professionals in the world! In 2009 MORI reported that 86% of people believe teachers can be trusted (in the context that nowadays only 29% of people believe that other people can be trusted compared with 60% 30 years ago). It is therefore very important that as Headteachers and teachers we do nothing to abuse the trust that the public places in us. On average 95% of people respond positively to a culture of trust whereas a minority will not and may continue to gossip, criticize and act in their own interests instead.

trust is a key factor in success

As Heads we can sometimes focus too much time on these mistrusting individuals rather than the 95% of positive people in the organisation.

brilliant tip

It is realistic to expect that some members of staff will have difficulty aligning themselves to the school's vision and will elect to move on. As Heads we can often encourage such staff to do so in an appropriate and supportive way.

Emotional intelligence

There are persuasive viewpoints stating the importance of emotional intelligence in successful leadership. An empathetic school leader will take genuine, heartfelt joy in the success of those around them because they work with a moral purpose focusing on the best interests of the learners in their care. At yoga classes, participants are naturally positive about seeing another participant out-performing them. A school undoubtedly works most effectively when similarly everyone is energised by the exceptional performance or expertise of others and it is important that as Headteachers we avoid a counter-productive blame culture. Emotionally intelligent schools possess 'hearts and brains' that embody optimism, drive, affection, care and compassion.

If the ethos is right then improvement is more likely; a consistency of approach combined with an air of relentless enthusiasm to change ensures success. Once compassion and emotional intelligence is in place in our schools we as Heads can confront more difficult issues ensuring that our moral purpose and school improvement remain at the forefront of our thinking and actions.

Leading change

In leading change Headteachers need to be able to make sense of what sometimes seem to be unconnected initiatives, diverse information and unrelated events in order to attempt to incorporate them into the school ethos and vision so that they become an integral part of the school improvement plans. Heads must also be the lead learner in the school, be mindful of health and safety issues, consider budget implications and legalities as well as the latest educational initiatives and thinking. Heads are expected to anticipate national educational changes incorporating them successfully into school even in the face of resistance.

Historically Heads and schools have had to deal with a furious pace of change and it is probably fair to assume that this is unlikely to abate in the years ahead. Heads need an endless supply of diplomacy and tact to achieve their school's vision within a climate of constant change. One of the key skills that Heads have had to acquire is the ability to choose the initiatives that will benefit their school and its aims and to disregard those that are irrelevant, no matter how strong the propaganda is that goes along with them!

brilliant dos and don'ts

Do

✔ Have a strong self-belief.

✔ Have endless optimism, work hard and avoid complacency.

✔ Be open, honest and frank.

Don't

✗ Never resort to bullying, humiliation or demoralising behaviour.

The lead learner

If as Heads we are the lead learner then part of our job is to read widely and be conversant with educational initiatives and changes so that we are secure in our beliefs and knowledge. This will ensure staff feel secure under our leadership and so will be more likely to accept change even when it is challenging. In addition to this part of our essential armoury we need to be good listeners and consult effectively so that when decisions are made there is a feeling of corporate ownership even when not everyone has agreed. We are at our most successful when we are ready to learn from our fellow professionals and are open-minded about change and new ideas. When faced with change a Head must continue to retain the clear moral purpose and set of strong values that they unswervingly role model and follow.

Distributed leadership

A school's leadership structure has its greatest influence on school performance and effectiveness when it is spread widely amongst trusted capable colleagues as well as within the leadership team. School leaders have the responsibility to improve teaching and learning and this can be most effectively done by improving staff motivation, encouraging a whole school commitment to the school's aims and by creating a comfortable, effective and stimulating environment. As leaders we collaboratively create a school vision and by involving staff in this process enable them to see a clear direction for the school. Key to a school's success is of course the quality of learning that is taking place, and a main focus for leaders must always be on improving staff performance through effective monitoring and support mechanisms such as a robust performance management system that looks to create the leaders of the future.

Succession planning must cultivate an ethos of alignment within the school; the whole school community sharing the same vision and therefore accepting the school's aims, goals and expectations. In the face of leadership change the school ethos will survive if its ownership is shared and deeply believed in. In the past Heads were appointed on the strength of their performance in the classroom and their curriculum knowledge rather than on leadership skills such as their charisma and ability to inspire the school community. Should the appointments and interview questions for headship therefore be geared to discovering what the candidate's people skills are and if they are emotionally intelligent as well as whether they have other key leadership skills?

With awareness of their own weaknesses Heads will often appoint staff to compensate for these areas. When a strong leadership team that has ownership of and decision-making powers over key responsibilities the Head's position will be strengthened rather than diminished. Heads can be likened to good referees: if a football game is going well you are totally unaware of the referee, you are barely aware of him or her being on the pitch and when the game is over the credit goes to the players for producing a wonderful game. The parallel with schools is that when something has been successful, the Head may have facilitated it and indirectly and skilfully led it but when success arrives it is the staff who believe they are responsible for it. Heads learn to be flexible rather than dogmatic in decision making whilst being resilient in the pursuit of high standards and achievement for all, both staff and pupils.

> Heads can be likened to good referees

Leading into the future

As Heads we must not allow ourselves to become totally consumed with the present; an important aspect to our job is to look into the future and have a clear vision of school development. Heads need plenty of time not only to lead but to reflect.

Managing the school is an essential part of the job but we all recognise the danger of it becoming all-consuming. In many schools the term 'management' has been replaced by the word 'leadership', clearly articulating the role of the senior team in leading the school to greater and greater success. The structure of the leadership team must reflect this aim with a strong team of senior, middle and curriculum leaders that share the school vision and are truly accountable to the Head and the Governing Body.

brilliant case study

The leadership team is centrally involved in the pupil-tracking process and can talk confidently about staff and pupils in the team. It is not one person that analyses the tracking and feeds back to staff and other interested parties but the teacher who knows their class's progress and knows which children need targeting to catch up and which need to be extended. The Team Leader knows their phase of school at every level and the curriculum leader knows all about their subject area and which element of the school is making the best or the weakest progress, what they are doing about it and finally what impact their actions are having.

All of this knowledge comes together at weekly leadership meetings and in termly structured feedback meetings. In the latter, curriculum and phase leaders look for common ground in their findings when they feed back to the Deputy Heads. Finally a collective report combining all the findings is verbally reported back to the Head.

The potential downfall of the distributed leadership model is that the Head is at the end of the line in terms of feedback and so is last to know what is happening, but this is avoided by discussions that take place at weekly leadership team meetings. The combined findings of these meetings, collated by the Head, are shared with the Chair of Governors weekly and later at full Governor Meetings and Governor Committee meetings until they ultimately find their way into the schools Self-Evaluation Form (see Figure 3.2).

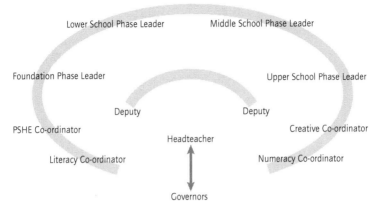

Figure 3.2 Leadership structure

The knowledge accumulated through distributed leadership enables Heads to confidently look into the future and make decisions on action needed to take the school forward. One of our most valuable strategies as Heads is the ability to listen and to ask pertinent, challenging and relevant questions that hold people accountable and help to progress the school; the Head as an enabler and with the ability to make successful appointments. It is said that Barack Obama deliberately appointed his challengers so that he was questioned on all of his decisions. Heads must appoint people that complement each other and not simply people in their own likeness, for when was the last time that anyone learnt anything through acquiescence?

Autocratic leadership

Some leaders like to make all key decisions themselves, keeping a close eye on employees, and there may be certain difficult situations or times when this approach is needed, for example during Special Measures. However autocratic leadership cannot be effective in the long term as disempowered staff will be demotivated to the point where their performance in the classroom is affected.

Consultative leadership

Some leaders take a much more consultative approach focusing on staff well-being and making decisions that are in everyone's best interests. The most democratic style of leadership is when trust is put in senior leaders and staff, actively encouraging them to make decisions whereby authority is truly delegated effectively due to good communication and clear accountability. Consultative leadership also helps succession planning. Empowerment and consultation are traits of the successful school but Heads will judge who they feel confident in empowering, who is not yet ready for leadership and who simply does not want the responsibility. Furthermore Heads must decide which decisions to make by themselves in isolation, which will be made in consultation with senior leaders, which can be made by someone else and which decisions need to be consulted upon with the whole staff.

Schools are now big businesses, held accountable for their outcomes in the same way as in the corporate world, with budgets to manage, data to analyse, people to advise, develop and on occasions to admonish and challenge about their performance. There are safeguarding, health and safety issues to be accountable for, child protection issues to address and legal issues to be aware of as well as curriculum matters to deal with to do with learning and teaching. No longer can Heads realistically deal with every aspect of the job.

More than ever before a Head's role, particularly in a large primary or secondary school, can be seen as the school equivalent of the industrial chief executive meaning management as well as leadership skills need to be of the highest order. In such circumstances emphasis rests on the collective working together rather than individuals working in isolation.

an autocratic Head is very likely to lead a dysfunctional school

If a Head works alone, makes all key decisions and ignores the team then it will not be long before they will be even more isolated, as will their staff. An autocratic Head is very likely to lead a dysfunctional school.

For the Head of a small primary school the challenges are no less significant, just different. Small village schools may have a Headteacher who teaches and a Secretary who is the Teaching Assistant. In a large primary the Head will not have a teaching responsibility and nor may the Deputy; in a large secondary there may be more leadership staff who have a high percentage of the week away from the chalk face or the interactive whiteboard. The role of the Site Manager, the Bursar or Finance Secretary and the Office Manager become invaluable cogs in the efficient running and management of the school. More and more as modern day Heads we are dependent upon the efficiency of these people and the talents and expertise of the leadership team and school staff to allow us to effectively lead our schools.

Theories and research

Steve Munby, the Chief Executive of the National College, talks of leadership as a service and being about 'what is best for the world not about being the best in the world'. In other words, it is not about 'what I want' as a leader but 'what is wanted of me'. Leadership is about the difference we make rather than our own self-importance. As Heads we serve the needs of the children, the community and the staff. He describes the leadership qualities of authentic leaders as being: developing others; the careful stewardship of resources; managing change; being a learner; being collaborative; being resilient; and holding courageous conversations.

As leaders we must have high expectations and hold people to account but as servant leaders we will also enjoy the success of others. Steve Munby goes on to say that 'the moral purpose' and the 'concept of service' must be at the heart of all we do as leaders. The leader is a 'vision keeper' who interprets the outside world to the inside world and this is ever more demanding in a world that is changing so much. So Munby rightly points out that one of the keys to successful leadership is knowing what to change and what to leave and crucially getting the timing of the change right.

Andy Hargreaves' book *The Fourth Way* describes how education and leadership within education have evolved over the past 30 years. He talks about successful leaders as ambitious and aspirational but that they are also humble, which falls into line with Steve Munby's description of leaders as servants. A common theme in leadership in a world that is changing so quickly is that we, as leaders, cannot have the answers to everything. We are operating, in the words of Ronald Heifetz, author of several books about leadership, 'at the frontier of our incompetencies' as we are in an adaptive society where the world is changing at a very fast rate. He argues that often people want leaders to have a technical answer to what is an adaptive situation that therefore does not have a known answer. As leaders we are often expected simply to direct, protect and keep or restore order but in our ever-changing world leaders nowadays often do not have the solution and are likely to ask questions as often as they give answers. Heifetz argues that solving technical problems is management whereas solving adaptive issues is leadership.

Good leaders, Hargreaves says, revel in their obstacles and great leaders do not wait for things to happen to them – they go out and happen to things. As leaders we need to have a vision, a commitment to a moral purpose and the ability to align others to the school's vision and ethos. Along the way we will always make mistakes but it is how we deal with a mistake that is important and we should never punish or be punished for honest mistakes. I also like Hargreaves' idea that good leaders creatively combine collaboration and competition. Often in the past they have been seen as opposites and yet I agree with Hargreaves that successful leadership does combine the two together successfully.

Bill Strickland the president and CEO of Manchester Bidwell in Pittsburgh has transformed the lives of thousands of disadvantaged children, young people and adults by simply believing that beautiful environments create beautiful people and prison-like environments do indeed create villains. In his book *Make the Impossible Possible* he simply declares that children deserve flowers, sunshine and hope, and talks about leadership and success being all about how you treat people. If you treat people and children as assets not as liabilities, and treat them as human beings, then those you help can achieve anything. He believes that the environment drives the behaviour and that buildings and galleries that create beautiful art, create beautiful people. We can be certain that our job as leaders has a great deal to do with how we deal with and interact with our school communities.

 **brilliant** recap

The role of headship has undoubtedly become more challenging over the years and nowadays involves a very wide range of tasks to master and lead. Not only must we behave with integrity and consistency, we must also inspire trust, have the skills to be creative and innovative as well as the courage to challenge orthodoxy and at times authority. As Heads we can shape the futures of the staff and children in our care and so can effectively transform people's lives. Over a career this can amount to thousands of people's lives!

We must be able to inspire trust amongst the school community, we must lead change, inspire and manage middle leaders in line with the school vision so that they inspire other staff, ensure a high quality of teaching and learning, respond to the pupil voice and align the staff and wider school community to the agreed priorities, aims and ethos of the school.

As Heads we must embody all the principles that are at the heart of the school's ethos. If we are seen as an authentic ambassador for the school, we will be successful and respected. As Heads we must also be good at managing. In other words we must master the operational activities that ensure that the organisation runs smoothly and effectively. Leadership is more about 'being' whereas management is more about 'doing'.

The factors that make a brilliant leader or Headteacher are many and complex. The world of education is full of theories and research which analyses the competencies that we need as Heads.

CHAPTER 4

Managing a school

Managing is showing people what to do; leading is showing people what direction to go in.

t may be that a Head's main focus is primarily around leadership issues but a school needs to be managed efficiently as well. Do we have to naturally possess the qualities of a good manager or can we learn? I would guess that for most of us it is a combination of both the instinctive and the learnt. Sir Alex Ferguson, one of the most successful football managers of all time, reached the top of his profession due to a combination of his natural personality traits, experience and good training. We may not want to manage our schools in the same style as Sir Alex manages Manchester United but we can learn about styles of management from him as well as other managers and colleagues in all walks of life. There is undoubtedly plenty for us to learn about with regard to management as most of us will have been trained as teachers in a classroom not as managers of a business, but research shows that Heads are often found to be some of the best managers from any walk of life.

Managing resources

Heads must provide the school with good value for money in respect of its human and physical resources; our schools will be inefficient if they are not resourced well according to the needs of the children. Resource needs for each school will vary but politicians and governments have given the impression that they would love a 'one-size fits all' recipe, not just in terms of resources but in terms of curriculum and management as well!

Even with ultimate perseverance as we search for such a utopia, it will not be discovered because all schools, their communities and their children are different and so the way Heads manage their schools must also be unique. However, a school needs to create its own management structure that caters for its own particular needs (*see Figure 4.1*).

Headteachers are not travelling along a predetermined conveyor belt transporting their clients to a successful conclusion. Education is not about simply adding bits of prescribed information, resources or approaches to produce well-rounded, responsible and successful children or schools.

brilliant tip

Headteachers must be continually responsive and sensitive to the particular needs of their school, the children, the staff and the community they serve and respond accordingly to those needs so that the school's vision, management and practice reflects the needs of all its stakeholders on a day-by-day and week-by-week basis. This demands careful and thoughtful management skills.

Managing change

In serving a school and its community a Head must introduce and manage change, the least popular of which is often imposed by higher authority. Those of us who have been in post since the last century have seen countless imposed national initiatives, some of which were not in our school's or our children's best interest, yet we have been obliged to implement the change. Experience of headship brings the ability to discern the relevant changes to implement and the confidence not to implement others that we see as irrelevant. For a less experienced Head this decision making can be a significant challenge. Whatever the circumstance, when change is imminent, Heads

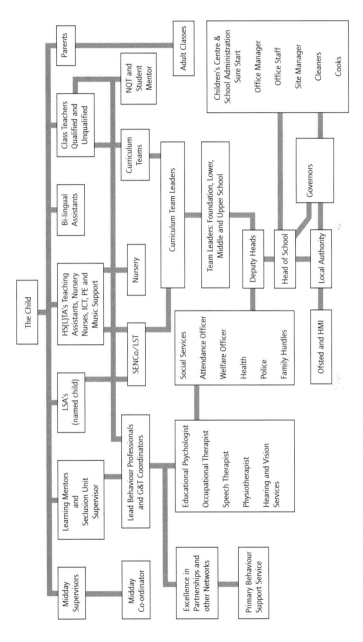

Figure 4.1 The school management structure

must display the qualities of optimism, energy and endless enthusiasm!

The historical context of educational change

The historical context, since 1988, is worth reviewing and I have used the DCSF website as a good source for such information. These changes give us a context for managing learning and teaching in schools that is relevant right up to the present day.

In August 1988, a paradigm shift in education occurred. The educational world changed with the introduction of what many people refer to as Kenneth Baker's Education Reform Act – the national curriculum. It was the most significant piece of education legislation since the Second World War and the 1944 Education Reform Act. The Education Reform Act became law and led to politicians and civil servants rather than educationalists dominating the decision making about how pupils are taught, right down to dictating the format of a lesson and for how many minutes you taught each element of a lesson. The Act also meant that anyone who aspired to manage changes in their school had the tools to do it with and could make a name for themselves in the process. 1988 saw the introduction of national curriculum tests to be taken by children at the ages of 7, 11 and 14, the prospect of inspections every six years, with published reports on schools and the advent of the controversial league tables.

From this date, known to many as the era of centralisation, as the DCSF website (www.dcsf.gov.uk) outlines for us:

Heads took greater financial responsibility for their schools and some Headteachers took the opportunity of their schools becoming a grant-maintained school so freeing them from their local authority. This new era witnessed the introduction of specialist, academy and faith schools. The 1988 Education Reform act led to the creation of the National Curriculum Council and the School Examinations and Assessment Council, the School Curriculum and Assessment Authority (CAA) and in 1997, SCAA merged with the National Council for Vocational Qualifications to form the Qualifications and Curriculum Authority and since 1988, the Secretary of State has responsibility for planning and directing the work of these bodies.

This new educational system, full of government-led educational reforms, resulted in the education system becoming like an examination factory but it has given Heads, Deputy Heads and schools the opportunity to manage quite radical changes in schools. In more recent times we have seen a review of the primary curriculum get underway in 2008/09 and, in 2008, a new secondary curriculum arrived. Fourteen- to 19-year-olds began to have access to a range of new specialised diplomas. Revised GCE A Levels began to be introduced and some schools have led curriculum reforms from within their own schools, so giving the brave and the creative another chance to make their names as managers and leaders of change. In 2010 the then new government introduced the opportunity for schools to apply for Academy status and in so doing release themselves for Local Authority control.

History suggests that if it is not an 'era of centralisation' then education will always be a land of opportunity for we will always be part of an 'era of change'. Within this historical context, outlined in more detail on the DCSF website, it is easy to see the opportunities for someone to lead and manage the Learning and Teaching in schools.

> education will always be a land of opportunity

The other significant issues that Heads must consistently manage, in terms of change, are pupil and staff turnover and long-term staff illness. This kind of change and its consequent impact on continuity provides a challenge for all of us who manage a school necessitating endless energy, optimism and a smile that never fades, even in the face of adversity! Managing change is part of the job; change is undoubtedly the one constant thing in education.

🡕 brilliant case study

Managing a challenging situation

When I knew that we were due an Ofsted inspection I decided to ask the Local Authority to implement a two-day inspection to help us with our monitoring and evaluation. The previous years SATs results both at KS1 and particularly at KS2 were very disappointing and there had been tears in the staffroom when we announced them as staff felt they had worked so hard. The following year's results were to be very good and the year after that the best we had ever had as a school, but we could not see into the future at the time, even though our tracking suggested we were going to improve. Much as we dislike the testing regime and the unreasonable level of importance that is placed on these results, they are a reality of life.

To lift spirits, make the staff feel better and to give them something to look forward to I requested a Local Authority monitoring inspection! As you can imagine this made me unpopular but it was needed and I decided it would avoid further and greater heartache in the future.

Ofsted is organised in regions and the lead inspector will have regular discussions with the Local Authority about the progress and support each school is making and receiving. Some Heads will not accept support and ideas from their Local Authority for a wide range of reasons which might include a lack of faith in their LA. However there is a real world and a bigger picture to consider and I knew that as our SATs results were not good enough, I needed to show that as a Head and as a school we were doing everything we could about the situation. When Ofsted did arrive or had discussions with the LA there needed to be a long list of action points that the school was undertaking to remedy the identified weaknesses and action points. Working with the LA was key to this for when they had their review meetings with the regional Ofsted Inspector I wanted them to be able to say that our school was willing to work alongside them and consider anything that might support their school improvement agenda.

One of the main issues that came out of this review was to look at the way we led and managed the school. I had been working towards a distributed leadership model. I had moved from myself as Head with two Assistant Heads to a much larger senior team that consisted of a Head, two Deputy Heads, four phase team leaders and two key curriculum team leaders for Literacy and Numeracy. In addition to this, one of the Deputy Heads was SENCo and I had another member of staff who took charge of NQT monitoring and student placements, the last two being jobs that I formally did. However, all of these roles were not as clear and defined as they could be. As a result when these staff members came to be interviewed by the LA, as Ofsted would do, they did not have all the answers because they did not have clear enough responsibilities and were not really being held fully accountable for what they were doing. The LA spotted this and we then negotiated a way forward. It meant greater responsibility and consequently workload for the middle managers but they wanted to be good at their jobs and welcomed the changes. The LA felt that the way we managed the school and the way we monitored could be better and more organised, with more formal feedback procedures. We followed the LA's advice and when Ofsted arrived, almost a year later, the new system was embedded and very effective. Indeed it came out as one of the strengths in the inspection report.

School as a business

Schools are in many respects a business (turnover can be between £2.5 and £3 million pounds a year in a large primary school and much more in a secondary school) so a great deal of thought must obviously be given to the financial management of a school. First of all a Head must delineate management issues from leadership issues; it is generally agreed that Heads need to spend more time on the latter than they often do. Management is mostly about completing tasks and often involves a lot of paperwork! Delegation of management issues comes back to making the right staffing appointments to the appropriate posts. If the school is not managed well, there will be less time available for the Head to think about leadership issues.

Delegation of duties

The management of many school issues falls upon the office staff. Many Heads appoint someone whose job it is to simply manage the budget, a Finance Secretary or Bursar who can make decisions, track the progress of the spending and meet with both Governors and the LA Financial Advisor (jobs that Heads traditionally did in the past). Regular Governor Finance Committee meetings can be led by this person and this means that the budget on a day-to-day basis is managed much more efficiently. The Head has ultimate responsibility so the employee is accountable to the Head and their performance and effectiveness must be monitored by the Head.

Office staff in larger schools are led by an Office Manager and another person manages attendance and yet another school dinners. The Office Manager reports to the Head and liaises with the Clerk to the Governors. All these roles must be accountable to their line manager and to the Head but most management issues do not need the Head's constant involvement. With trust and confidence in the abilities of office staff the Head need not be closely involved in such management tasks.

Managing the school timetable is a significant piece of work needing skilled engineering in larger schools where Heads may often take the lead. First-hand working knowledge of this and the management of PPA is invaluable, but other management issues such as student placements can be delegated as well as the monitoring of NQTs. Heads decide, based on their own individual circumstances, that which can safely be delegated.

Other areas in school that need managing include special needs, child protection, looked after children, gifted and talented provision, EAL provision, support staff, in-service training and learning mentors – the list is not exhaustive!

Continual professional development

Heads must be skilled at managing the development of staff and developing their competence in terms of leadership. This will include accessing continuous professional development (CPD) that can be provided internally through school-based experiences and expertise as well as externally. Skilfully managing the CPD needs of all staff, both teachers and those supporting, is crucial in terms of succession planning. We must of course give consideration to any budgetary financial constraints as well as seeking maximum impact from the individual CPD so that it has a benefit for the whole school. The establishment of a CPD network should be considered a school priority as collaborating with other schools is often a great way to further develop staff.

The school management structure

If they are not careful Heads can spend a lot of their time managing practicalities rather than strategically leading the school, so the organisation of an effective management structure is a key factor not only in terms of staff development but for the smooth running of the school and facilitation of the Head's leadership responsibilities. A school must have a staffing structure that formalises how we appoint and pay staff and that clarifies staffing responsibilities (see Figure 4.2). This structure will obviously vary from school to school, reflecting the size and needs of that school.

In terms of succession planning there is now a much more clearly defined staffing structure nationally that enables staff to develop and progress from one role in school to another and enables Heads to give opportunities for all staff to make decisions and develop themselves as leaders. We can create an ethos of staff development that includes the ability for staff to feel safe to fail as part of that learning and development process. There is of course a school/establishment hierarchy that has to be followed and respected and certain protocols must be followed within the school's leadership structure. We have an obligation to manage the professional development of our staff and as part of this we need to take succession planning very seriously indeed. One of the most satisfying aspects of the job is to develop an NQT into a leading teacher, a team leader, a Deputy Head and then watch them move on to headship. Hopefully they are better than we are by the end of the process, no longer needing us as they make their own way!

> we need to take succession planning very seriously indeed

Like the Learning Support Assistant who watches her charges develop so well that they become independent of her, as Heads we have equally succeeded in doing our job well.

Heads nowadays manage people, observe and rate lessons, and manage the budget and all other financial factors that result in a school providing good value for money. It is important that we have a background in teaching and have taught regularly in the classroom, but it is most important that we do our job of managing and leading the school well.

Head of School (L28–L34)
Budget, staffing, timetabling, inset, governor, parent, community liaison, SIP threshold, performance management leader, newsletters, monitoring and evaluating, curriculum overview responsibilities, health & safety, child protection, student placements

Deputy Head (L11–15)
Responsibility for assessment, including marking and reporting to parents across the whole school, coordinate stats, + QCA testing throughout the school. Monitoring and evaluating, performance management leader, school council coordinator, curriculum overview responsibilities, G&T coordinator, lead behaviour professional

60% Deputy Head/Senco (L11–15)
SEN, child protection, looked after children, teaching assistants, monitoring and evaluating, performance management leader

Foundation School Leader (Years N and R) TLR 2 (+£3,750)
Responsibility for the foundation stage (including discipline matters), monitoring and evaluating, performance management leader

Lower School Leader (Years 1 and 2) TLR 2 (+£3,750)
Responsibility for the lower school (including discipline matters), monitoring and evaluating, performance management leader

Middle School Leader (Years 3 and 4) TLR 2 (+£3,750)
Responsibility for the middle school (including discipline matters), monitoring and evaluating, performance management leader

Upper School Leader (Yrs 5 and 6) TLR 2 (+£3,750)
Co-ordinate the running of upper school (including discipline matters), monitoring and evaluating, performance management leader

Nursery TLR 2 (+£2,250)
Nursery Staff
SEN

NQT Coordinator TLR 2 (+£2,250)
Newly Qualified Teachers Mentor

Learning Support Teacher (SEN) TLR 2 (+£3,750)
Teaching assistants

Student Coordinator TLR 2 (+£2,250)
Student mentor

Mathematics Leader TLR 2 (+£2,250)

PSHE Leader TLR 2 (+£2,250)

Science Leader TLR 2 (+£2,250)

Class Teachers FTE (21 class bases)
Performance management and curriculum leaders (unqualified / M1–M6 / UP Levels)

Topic Leader TLR 2 (+£2,250)

English Leader TLR 2 (+£2,250)

HLTAs (8) to cover for teaching staff absence (Grade 9) and involved in planning
higher level PE assistant: cover for PPA (Grade 9)
higher level music assistant: cover for PPA (Grade 9) (12)

HSTAs (8) to cover for teaching staff absence
nursery nurses (2.2 FTE) support in the nursery, covering class (Grade 7)

Teaching assistants who support named children. (Grade 6) posts vary according to number of named children on medical or priority 4 hours and statements

Teaching/bilingual assistants (Grade 6), class room support, (Rec.– Yr 6)
1 × **ICT support assistant** (Grade 5)
nursery manager: Grade 9
nursery assistant manager: Grade 8
nursery assistants: Grade 6 (7)

Higher level learning mentor (1): (Grade 9)
performance management leader and involved in planning

Midday Coordinator (1) and **Midday Supervisors** (22) (Grade 4)

Learning mentors × 2 (Grade 6)
Seclusion Unit Supervisor (Grade 8).

Office Manager (1), (Grade 9)   **Finance Secretary** (1), (Grade 8)   **Admin. Assistants** (2) (Grade 6)

Site Manager (1), (Grade 8)

Cleaners (8), (Grade 3)

Caterer (1)   **Catering assistants** (3)

Figure 4.2 A staffing structure for a school including salary gradings, responsibilities and number of staff

 **brilliant** recap

Although leadership is vitally important we know that a school will not run efficiently unless it is managed well. What makes a good leader or manager? For many it is someone who can inspire and get the most from their staff.

There are many qualities that are needed to be a good manager and they overlap with those of a good leader. A Head needs to have excellent interpersonal skills; of communicating his or her view clearly as well as also being a good listener. On a practical level, a good manager needs to be knowledgeable and well-informed about all educational and school matters. A good manager has a certain presence that communicates an air of authority and can make decisions whilst remaining calm, even in a pressured situation. Managers need to be ambitious and able to think creatively as well. As managers we should delegate effectively and then hold staff appropriately accountable.

As managers we deal with each of our employees in different ways just as good teachers do not treat all of their pupils in the same way. Sometimes it may be necessary to be firm with certain staff, whilst other staff will respond to a more relaxed approach. As Heads we can develop a system to manage the school so effectively that we will then give ourselves enough time to fulfil our primary role, which is to lead the school strategically. The approach may vary even with the same person and it may be a combination of the two, but one thing is for certain, whatever approach is taken, a school is only as good as the person managing it.

CHAPTER 5

Challenging
situations

This chapter looks at the issues involved in identifying and dealing with difficult situations that may cause Heads to have sleepless nights, such as dealing with a school in Special Measures, deficit budgets, staff redundancy, capability procedures, breaches of contract, unprofessional conduct, vandalism, difficult parents and badly behaved pupils. We will look at these difficult situations within the context of how to make the best of them and I will elaborate by explaining the support I have had. In such circumstances support can come from Governors, Chair of Governors, Deputy Heads, the Local Authority and an understanding family – but ultimately, of course, the decisions and resolutions have to be made by the Head! I have had to face and deal with all of the situations listed above and sometimes with more than one concurrently.

brilliant example

It's March and the third new year, not counting Chinese New Year, is about to start (after the new school year in September comes the calendar New Year in January and then in bronze medal position is the financial New Year in April). Optimism is plentiful: the summer term approaches, spring is brightening our world with the prospect of longer days and warmer weather when the children will access the school field and enjoy nature.

The school I am working in should be coming out of Special Measures after our May visit and then … The poor financial situation that the Local Authority had agreed need not be dealt with during Special Measures must now be sorted out so redundancy looms, and we discover that the Deputy Head looks as if he will lose his job and I must now deal with what became a year-long unprofessional conduct issue before its final conclusion at a formal hearing held by the former General Teaching Council. In addition, there is no doubt that the teacher at the end of the corridor who has failed every lesson observation by the school, HMI and the LA will now have to go down the capability route if children's educational progress is not to be further damaged and then Keith, my favourite Inspector, starts his final visit and observes what he describes as the worst PE lesson that he has ever seen.

Surprisingly I now look back on it all and realise that in dealing with all these issues how much stronger it made me and how I am undoubtedly a better Head because of all these experiences.

Special Measures

Failing a school Ofsted inspection is probably the number one fear for any Headteacher. The Ofsted website (www.ofsted.gov. uk) will tell you primary schools that require Special Measures vary in size, type and socio-economic circumstances, going on to say that a common denominator in failing schools is very low standards of achievement and comparatively lower levels in National Curriculum tests than those found in similar schools. Other failure parameters, outlined by Ofsted on their website, are poor teaching and weak leadership, the continuing existence of weaknesses identified in previous inspections, poor pupil behaviour and lack of engagement in lessons and a lack of decisive action on key school improvement areas. To avoid failing an inspection it is important that a Head has high expectations about what pupils can achieve, makes sure that lesson planning is good and that there is a wide range of classroom activities available to engage pupils in their learning. In schools with unsatisfactory leadership, there is often no clear direction and so as Heads we must ensure effective monitoring of all aspects of the school's work and instigate thorough evaluation of the impact of change.

The Head of a school that is subject to Special Measures will have regular short-notice Ofsted inspections to monitor its improvement. Heads and Governors must take strong and decisive action in all the areas that a school has been identified as underperforming and to support this HMI will write a report after each visit with agreed short-term targets. If intervention is unsuccessful, then the leaders and teaching staff can lose their jobs, the school Governors can be replaced and ultimately, if the school fails to improve, it may be closed.

Before the Education Act of 2005, failing schools were put into Serious Weaknesses and, if no improvement was forthcoming, were put into Special Measures. Since the Act, failing schools are given a notice to improve and re-inspected after one year. When a school is placed in Special Measures, it has to devise an action plan highlighting the key areas it needs to develop as identified by the inspection team and the school must meet agreed targets in order to leave the category. The progress of the action plan is monitored by HMI who visit the school once a term for one or two days to evaluate progress. The visit may be unannounced. Once the HMIs are satisfied that the action plan has been satisfactorily addressed Ofsted will return and inspect the school again. If the Ofsted team agree with HMI's judgement, the school is then removed from the Special Measures category.

When schools are in Special Measures they usually receive well-focused support from the inspecting team that will visit termly and the Local Authority link advisor who will have an important role in providing or organising appropriate training for staff, including the school leaders. With such support, progress and improvement usually follow. In this situation, as Heads we should be proactive in ensuring that the LEA takes swift, supportive action and we should ensure that the monitoring of teaching and learning secures better results and improved classroom practice.

brilliant tip

Involving parents in helping the school to improve is a good strategy as often in failing schools there is poor attendance, poor punctuality and little support for homework. Primary and secondary schools in difficult circumstances often have parents who take term-time holidays and are not concerned about their child's regular absence from school. By introducing meetings with the parents of pupils for whom attendance is a concern together with introducing fines for families who take holidays in term time, the Head can make explicit to the whole school community the school's policy and practice with regard to attendance.

Capability

EPM (Education Personnel Management), the Huntingdon-based personnel advisors that our school uses, explain the process clearly in their policies and guidance. If an employee's performance and progress against agreed targets is consistently less than satisfactory the Head must begin by discussing the issues with them as specifically as possible, and in the case of a teacher this may involve the team leader responsible for the teacher's performance review under the school's performance management policy. Structured information and systematic recording will inform the discussion and the employee will be given a reasonable opportunity to comment and explain. In the course of these discussions further appropriate targets will be set and any appropriate professional development (in-service training, visits to other schools, discussion with appropriate colleagues or professionals) will be considered and planned. EPM also makes it clear that the employee will be informed that their performance will be monitored over an identified and specified period, usually no more than six weeks. A shorter timescale may be appropriate if the concerns over capability pose a real risk to the health, safety or well-being of children, or is likely to result in serious damage to pupils' education. In extreme cases, the Headteacher may decide to initiate formal procedures immediately.

> the Headteacher may decide to initiate formal procedures immediately

The more serious the lack of capability the shorter the timescale will be to achieve targets as the children's welfare must be of paramount importance. If progress is not forthcoming an oral warning would be the first step that is taken and then formal procedures would be followed as outlined in the school's discipline policy. A written warning must be issued before a final warning, which can then lead to dismissal and consequent appeals, if the member of staff's progress against targets is not 'wholly satisfactory'. Effectively this would mean a teacher would never get a job in education again.

brilliant tip

The result of a capability procedure can often be demoralising for staff throughout the school. A Head needs to be sensitive to this but must always hold the children's best interests at heart, knowing that their actions will, in the long run, improve outcomes for children.

Difficult parents

From time to time as Heads we will be faced with an angry parent: such situations can be difficult, upsetting and time consuming. Parents will usually get upset if they think that their child is being bullied, treated unfairly or is not doing as well as they think they should be regarding their educational progress. As Heads we might find that either the parent is mistaken or that they are fully justified! The Head must always be clear to staff and parents that their first priority is the child's best interests and overall welfare. We want the best for every child in our school. If this is the perception parents have of our school leadership then usually a problem can be amicably sorted. In such difficult encounters the key is to stay calm, be patient and show concern. Be positive and focus on the child's good qualities whilst addressing the issue, as later you may have to deal with the child being at fault, so sensitively pave the way for this possible eventuality.

brilliant tip

If the child and the family have a track record of being difficult then keep a record of each meeting you have with the family and also be proactive. If you see a problem arising then anticipate it and call the parents in before they come storming in. Approach the meeting fully informed about the child and how they are doing in school both academically and socially. Allow the parents to ask questions and share concerns and offer them support. If you are unsure of anything, do not respond immediately but promise to come back to them at an agreed later date. If the parent becomes aggressive and confrontational then bring the meeting to an immediate end and arrange one at a later date. Always be prepared for the worst and be prepared in case parents make a formal complaint. Take minutes of any meetings that take place, 'if it is not written down – it never happened', and always see parents with other staff present to witness what happens and what is said. A bonus to such situations is that staff will gain in experience by observation.

Dealing with difficult parents can be one of the hardest parts of the job. For our own personal sanity as Heads we need to be good at focusing on the positive issues as they far outweigh the difficult situations.

Deficit budgets and redundancy

As staff salaries represent at least 80% of almost every school's budget then redundancy is the inevitable consequence of a deficit budget and in such circumstances it is necessary to follow the LA's policy and procedure. Heads would be well advised not to act alone but to contact the school's personnel advisors and of course the school Governors. In the event that it is necessary to make a reduction in staff, the governing body, having consulted with the personnel committee it has appointed, will inform all the staff concerned and the trade unions involved of the following (taken from the Education Personnel Management (EPM) website and policy):

(a) *the reasons for the redundancy.*

(b) *the number and descriptions of the employees to be dismissed as redundant.*

(c) *the total number of employees of any such description employed at the school.*

(d) *the proposed method of selecting the employees to be dismissed.*

(e) *the proposed method of carrying out the dismissals, including the period over which the dismissals are to take effect.*

(f) *the method of calculating any compensation to be paid to redundant employees.*

(www.epm.co.uk)

The selection criteria are determined by the Headteacher in consultation with the Chair of Governors who will then consult with the trade unions.

brilliant tip

To try and avoid compulsory redundancies, reduction can be achieved by:

- natural turnover and staff resignations
- deletion of vacancies
- voluntary redeployment of staff into other suitable posts within the school
- voluntary transfer to part-time working
- reduced hours or job sharing arrangements
- voluntary redundancy
- termination of appointment of staff over the normal retirement age and a review of any fixed-term contracts.

The governing body decides if any requests for voluntary redundancy can be accepted in which case an offer will be made to the employee in question identifying the level of compensation they could expect.

EPM go on to explain that if the necessary staffing reduction is not achieved by any of the above means then the Headteacher will, following the consultative process, meet individually with staff identified as at risk, to hear representations from the individual as to why they should not be selected. Individuals will be given due notice of the meeting in writing and will be entitled to be accompanied by a trade union representative or a friend.

Following these meetings the Headteacher and the Dismissal Committee will make the selection on the basis of all the information available and in line with the identified selection criteria. The employee(s) selected will be informed in writing that the Headteacher will recommend to the Dismissal Committee, also known as the First Committee (the panel or committee set up by a fully quorate governing body with delegated power to dismiss) that the employee(s) be dismissed on grounds of redundancy. However, in most schools the power to dismiss has been delegated to the Head, so that Governors are then used as the 'higher authority' to which an appeal can be made. This has implications for Deputy Heads and senior leaders in schools as they will then find themselves having to handle the conduct or capability process which would include the issuing of formal warnings, as the Head is not allowed to be involved in the process: they are ultimately responsible for dismissing the member of staff. The obvious implication of this is that senior leaders will need to undergo training in this process. Following the stages above the member of staff to be made redundant can then appeal against the decision, if they wish to.

> the power to dismiss has been delegated to the Head

The Appeals Panel will consist of at least the same number of Governors who made the decision to dismiss and who have played no part in the selection of the employee(s) for dismissal on the grounds of redundancy.

Once again, like other such difficult situations, redundancy will have a negative affect on staff well-being and morale. There is no easy way round this and as Heads we need to be very sensitive, totally fair and legally correct, consulting personnel advisors and Governors at every stage of the process. Despite the level of consultation involved in making a post redundant, staff often take redundancy decisions as a personal attack. Therefore best practice is to approach redundancy procedures with a longer-term vision of the school's finance in order to avoid stressful repetition of the whole process within a relatively short timescale.

Unprofessional conduct/breaches of contract

It is important that school leaders model appropriate conduct and behaviour demonstrating the policy that will be in place for staff regarding acceptable professional boundaries. Unprofessional conduct or a breach of contract is usually the result of someone 'abusing what should be respectful, caring and professional relationships between adults and pupils through a lack of integrity, maturity or good judgement but accusations from a child, parent or member of staff can also be malicious, false or mistaken' (www.epm.co.uk). The Head, with the support of Governors and the school's personnel advisor, must address the situation appropriately.

Issues of unprofessional conduct usually mean that a member of staff has behaved in a way that has harmed, or may have harmed a child, possibly committing a criminal offence, indicating their unsuitability to work with children. This constitutes a serious abuse of trust by the staff member.

brilliant tips

A successful Head must ensure appropriate policies and guidance are in place to advise their staff clearly that:

- They must not put themselves in a vulnerable situation with pupils who may have got infatuated with a member of staff.
- They need to take care not to accept any gift that might be construed by others as a bribe, or lead the giver to expect preferential treatment.
- The use of social networking sites can put staff in very vulnerable positions if they use them to communicate with children.
- They should avoid situations where they are alone with a pupil as this could be misconstrued.

- The Head's clear guidance must be followed with respect to educational visits, after school clubs or in cases where pupils may need transporting by car from one place to another.

- Use of the internet, photography and filming must be carefully monitored.

(From EPM policies, www.epm.co.uk)

Vandalism

Heads must assess their school's unique circumstances in order to plan and budget appropriately to address the threat of vandalism.

The research that I have read about school vandalism suggests that there are generally four types of vandalism – nuisance, malicious, professional and, less likely, ideological. Most school vandals are teenagers who have often been suspended, excluded or who are truants and they are usually male. Their motive can be vindictive towards a particular member of staff but equally likely is the simple motive of amusement. Many schools have sophisticated security camera systems, outside lights, alarm systems or even security firms patrolling the grounds. A more proactive, preventative approach might include arranging sports activities, arts activities, youth clubs, educational programmes, alcohol and drug awareness programmes, and restorative justice programmes to involve the community in the school and in so doing make the school a valued part of its community.

School vandalism is quite often connected to a societal problem and so Heads benefit by building relationships with the local community which will become more protective of the school thus reducing the likelihood of it being vandalised. Of course schools suffer from internal vandalism as well that can be wilful and malicious. In such instances it is hoped that parents and teachers would rally together against the perpetrators and as Heads we can contact the police so that they investigate the crime. Vandalism can have rippling effects throughout an entire school community; insurance claims levied, upset members of the school community and high repair costs.

When it happens vandalism can impact on the emotions of the whole school community and so as Heads we must be prepared to be the steady rock upon which the whole school relies and depends.

Behaviour management

In school a Head's job is to make sure that everyone feels safe, is able to learn and is treated with respect.

All staff, and most significantly the Head, are role models; staff and children look up to the Head for a lead, everything we do is scrutinised, interpreted or even misinterpreted! The former General Teaching Council (GTC) introduced a Code of Conduct that controversially said teachers should be aware of their actions, behaviours and lifestyles, 24 hours a day. It could be construed as idealistic but the GTC promoted that Heads must ensure every aspect of their lives promotes what is morally and ethically correct. It is probably fair to assume that most parents have traditional expectations of Headteachers and behaving inappropriately is not what they want to see their child's Head doing. We have chosen to be professional educators who should therefore earn the children's and parents' respect. Our role is clear and we are professionals who are not and cannot be the children's friend or entertainer, nor can or should we be their substitute parent. We can and should be exemplary role models for those who want someone to look up to.

> most parents have traditional expectations of Headteachers

Whole school approach to behaviour

Research shows that if anything is to be successful in a school it needs the full support and enthusiasm of the Head who must be seen to be taking an active lead. In terms of behaviour management this is crucial because the only behaviour management strategies that are going to truly work are the ones that follow a common whole school approach, led by the Head. It is an obvious thing to say but children are not going to learn if teaching and learning are hindered by poor behaviour. It is equally important that Heads strive to ensure their teachers' main focus in the classroom is learning rather than behaviour management.

In some schools behaviour management hinges on the Head or Senior Leadership Team but as Heads we should secure a team approach. The Head is always there as an ultimate sanction but to be successful there need to be common approaches from class to class and year group to year group so that the majority of behaviour issues are dealt with by the member of staff who is on the front line at the time. Misbehaviour should be dealt with in line with agreed school behaviour management strategies. All staff must take responsibility for behaviour within their class but if they see a child from another class misbehaving they must also deal with it.

brilliant tip

Heads take the lead agreeing with their school community what strategies work in their school. Just as there is not one curriculum approach that will work in all schools equally there is not one set behaviour management approach that will work in every school. However there are certain common principles, approaches and practices that are common to schools that manage behaviour well.

Extreme behaviour

Heads can face, in some schools, children who cannot be kept in the classrooms but who are found wandering the corridors, the playground, the field or leaving the school grounds altogether. Behaviour, when it is out of control, can result in pupils being found under tables, flicking pencils and rubbers, as well as indulging in every variety of lower level disruption that you could name. In extreme situations pupils will swear, regularly fight each other and even attack members of staff and can deliberately damage school property. Incidents of bullying and racism can dominate the playground with children and staff being subjected to aggressive, abusive behaviour. There is no underestimating how threatening and out of control pupils can become but it is also reassuring to know that the vast majority of schools and classes do not have these extreme situations to deal with.

brilliant example

In one school, every Friday afternoon, whilst all the well-behaved children had a half-hour extra playtime, the naughty ones would be sent to the Head, all together, in the hall, in silence, with nothing to do for 30 long, long minutes. During the week those same children (who perhaps needed more than any other children, to be running around the playground or the field, letting off steam after, in their eyes, being cooped-up in a classroom, behind a desk) were to be found standing outside the staffroom at break and lunch times facing the wall! The system was simply not working and everyone blamed the children rather than the system.

brilliant tip

In all behaviour management approaches Heads must ensure that the bottom line is not only consistency in approach but also fairness. Heads can consult with staff and pupils to arrive at a whole school approach to behaviour management with agreed sanctions and rewards that are consistently applied by the whole staff. In the eyes of both staff and pupils it must be fair, but nothing is ever that simple. Some children need a hard line to conform and align to the school's approach and ethos whilst others will need support and even counselling. Despite having to apply the agreed school rules consistently across the school all pupils are different and will need catering for in subtly different ways if they are to be successfully managed within the school.

Exclusion

So for those of us in headship, with whom lies the ultimate responsibility for school safety, what is the process for correcting such extreme behaviour? The ultimate sanctions are fixed-term and permanent exclusions. Such a strategy can be effective but does not often sort out that pupil's poor behaviour, it simply passes it on to another school. However when a pupil has a long history of fixed-term exclusions and extreme behaviour, permanent exclusions can be the only solution. Some schools will enforce a zero tolerance approach to poor behaviour and may follow the baseball rule of three strikes and you are out.

Consistency and fairness

Heads and staff must be unrelentingly consistent as all pupils need to feel they are equally valued and appreciated and pupils, like staff, will recognise differences in other pupils and cater for them. Heads should strive to give equal time to all the pupils in their care but reality will mean that some pupils need more time than others; the vast majority of pupils will conform to an agreed set of rules and strategies. Whatever the need, whatever the individual's uniqueness, the agreed sanctions should be applied to all. With regard to behaviour management it is probably fair to say that a set recipe can rarely cater for all as all children and their circumstances are so different.

the agreed sanctions should be applied to all

Researchers say that for one in seven people school is a negative experience so as Heads we must ensure fairness by giving everybody what they need. Within that maxim it is important that schools do not tolerate any low-level disruption and that they consistently hold children accountable for poor choices, applying positive and negative consequences with consistency. Once again life is not simple and being caring means sometimes being prepared to make unpopular decisions for the greater good. Pupils and adults respect consistency and fairness, assertiveness not aggression; there should be no raised voices, no sarcasm and no put-downs. Essentially children like to be with people who like and respect them and in that context they will generally accept decisions that are made, even if they are not felt to be in their own best interests.

 **brilliant** recap

With great power comes great responsibility.

(Spiderman)

The job of headship is a very rewarding one but there is no escaping the fact that not all aspects of the job are to be relished. If we have the school ethos correct and staff, parents, pupils and the school community are feeling positive then a lot of the more difficult situations can be anticipated and even avoided if there is trust within the organisation and its wider community.

Often it is when we are facing the job's more difficult situations that we become very aware of the great responsibility of headship and solving the challenges and difficult situations can be one of the most rewarding aspects of the job.

CHAPTER 6

Working with parents and Governors

t is important for Heads to ensure that their schools enjoy the benefits of a close working partnership with both the parent body and the Governing Body. Parental, Governor and school community involvement in schools is an important factor in raising children's achievements and there is a great deal of research to show that when parents are involved with their child's education, children do better.

Working with parents

Governments (refer to www.teachernet.gov.uk) have justifiably tried to encourage parental involvement; as the teachernet website points out parents have the right to get involved in decision making at a school level, for example concerning school policy, or even at local authority level by challenging Local Authorities on the quality and range of schools available in their area. The views of parents on our schools are often some of the most accurate we can get and schools are now required to consider and act upon parents' views as part of a school's self-evaluation.

Communication

Effective communication with parents is an important ingredient of a successful school and it has to be a two-way process. By this I mean that parents need to have an understanding of the wide-ranging demands placed on teachers' time and their consequent work load. Essentially the whole school community needs to feel valued and it is equally important that as a profession we value the roles of others, but also that this respect is reciprocated. Parents may base their views of schooling on the experiences they had in education which can often be very different from those of their children. Furthermore the language and jargon used by schools about levels, attainments and curriculum will confuse parents as such terms did not exist in their school days. Schools need to be particularly sensitive in communicating appropriately with hard-to-reach parents who do not engage with their child's school and parents who have a special educational need themselves. Another hard-to-reach group is those families who have English as an additional language.

A significant aspect of working with parents is information sharing about children's performance. It is important to ensure parents get a holistic picture and that the focus is not too heavily weighted towards academic achievement. Parents are usually very concerned about their child's happiness at school and so the child's well-being, as well as academic progress, must be central to a school's reporting to parents process.

brilliant tip

One way we can be sure parents are well informed is to have a regular school questionnaire that asks parents about their level of satisfaction with issues that are relevant to their child's education; for example, the educational aims of the school, assessment, resources, school policy on behaviour, attendance, racism and bullying. A carefully worded questionnaire may highlight which groups of parents are in greatest need of information so allowing the school to adapt the information for individuals or groups.

Someone once half humorously said that there are three types of parent:

1. Those that do not care.

2. Those that take the whole thing seriously, but not too seriously.

3. Those that get just about everything out of proportion.

So how do we connect with all three groups? Regular communication with parents is important and often primary schools in particular allow parents to bring their children into school in the mornings resulting in a relaxed conversational start to the school day when parents and staff can communicate with each other – an open-door policy. A guaranteed way to alienate parents is to appear unavailable and unresponsive. If opportunities are available to meet in a formal and informal way then the more likely it is that issues will be resolved quickly. Parents need to feel secure and need to feel that they can trust school staff. There is no doubt that appropriate parental involvement can make a difference to the success of the children in our schools.

Support from parents

Parents can be a very effective resource if we can get them actively involved in their child's education. One simple way is to provide parents with ideas and activities they could do at home with their child and the use of school websites or VLEs (virtual learning environments) makes it a lot easier to provide such support than it was in the past.

brilliant tip

Communicating with parents can include writing a class newsletter, inviting parents into the classroom, phoning parents with good news about their child's progress, well done/celebration assemblies to which parents are invited, home visits at the start of a child's schooling, parents coming in as voluntary helpers, surveying parents about their interests and then enlisting their help as part of a school topic, organising parent support groups, running a breakfast club, inviting parents to help with extra-curricular clubs, having a home–school agreement, on-going progress reports on the VLE instead of a once a year summative report, keeping parents informed well in advance about curriculum coverage, events and trips, and making policies and information about the school easily available on the VLE or school website.

If we are being successful in working with parents then ideally we would hope that parents will provide a home environment that supports the development of their child's education, involve themselves in the life of the school, value the school's advice and support and share their concerns about their child openly. However, we must not be naïve, because many parents will surprise us with their complete lack of interest in their child's education and will prove to be very hard to reach in terms of altering such a perspective. This does seem to be a sad reality that we must face and then try to compensate for in the interests of the child.

Home–School agreements

Heads recognise that for the parent–school partnership to be effective there must be a shared commitment to collaboration, open lines of communication, mutual respect, and a common or shared vision. Schools must actively seek and value parents' views not only about their child but also the school as a whole. If children see that their parents are enthusiastic about their school they are more likely to engage in their learning and in the life of the school.

The government's guidelines on home–school agreements suggests the school asks these questions:

- *What do parents expect from the school?*
- *What does the school expect from parents?*
- *What do parents think of the school?*
- *How does the school involve parents in their child's education?*
- *Why do some parents not get involved?*
- *What can the school do to establish an effective working relationship with hard-to-reach parents?*
- *What can the school do to help parents to help their child?*
- *What priority does the school give to working with parents?*
- *What does the school do to listen to the views of pupils, parents and the school community?*

(www.standards.dcsf.gov.uk)

A welcoming school

There are some simple cosmetic things that we can do to create a welcoming school. We can ensure that the main entrance is well-signposted so that visitors and parents can find their way in easily and we can make sure the school entrance is both welcoming and informative. We can also ensure staff on the front desk are welcoming and friendly together with signage around the school so that we are continually reassuring parents and visitors that they are welcome. Office staff can ensure that issues are dealt with promptly and that concerns are reported back on. It is always a good idea to make sure we contact parents when there is good news, not just with bad. One excellent step forward that more and more schools are taking is personalising the letter home so that each family has its own name at the top. Another successful strategy to help adults feel welcome in the school is to encourage and organise daytime or out-of-school learning programmes for parents (Extended School and Children's Centre programmes can help with this sort of support). Inter-agency collaboration such as this may include enabling families to

contact parents when there is good news, not just with bad

work and liaise with adult education workers, social care, education welfare workers, health workers, the police and voluntary sector workers.

Working with Governors

Apart from children and their parents, the key people in the school community are obviously the staff and Governors. Classically we are told as Heads and staff that it is a priority to get on with the site manager, the secretary, the cook and the groundsman for very obvious practical reasons but it is necessary to add the Chair of Governors to that list as well. If a Head has an effective and supportive Chair of Governors, this critical friendship can make a significant difference.

What is a governing body?

An effective governing body:

- *Leaves day-to-day management to the Headteacher.*
- *Establishes the school's ethos, aims and objectives.*
- *Agrees the school budget and allocates resources.*
- *Reviews staffing structures.*
- *Sets objectives for the Headteacher and challenges them to drive improvement.*
- *Forms effective community partnerships.*
- *Receives, considers and challenges information provided by the school to monitor pupil progress, improvement and well-being.*
- *Reviews and agrees the self-evaluation form and is accountable to parents via the school profile.*

(From The 21st Century School: Implications and Challenges for Governing Bodies, DCSF, April 2010)

School Governors are a voluntary group that collectively makes strategic decisions about school development in terms of the premises, personnel issues, curriculum matters, financial progress and admissions. Governors meet as a full governing body and also as committees to cover the above areas. The governing body will comprise the Head, parents, Local Authority representatives as well as members of the community and the staff. The governing body will decide on the number of school Governors and how many will be represented in each of the groups above within certain parameters that are set out within the Local Authority's Governor Handbook. The governing body will also appoint a Clerk to the Governors which is a paid role. The Clerk is not part of the decision-making process. Governors are allowed 'reasonable' time off work to carry out their governor duties but it does not have to be paid time off.

Local Authorities provide training for Governors; Heads can actively encourage their Governors to attend to increase their understanding of the role. Training avoids Governors getting involved in day-to-day issues rather than focusing on bigger strategic issues. Local Authority training will provide Governors with advice on financial issues, Ofsted, their roles and responsibilities as well as training for the Clerk.

Peterborough's guidance to schools on governing bodies points out that:

there are five types of school: community schools, foundation schools, voluntary aided/controlled schools, community special schools and foundation special schools. In community schools the Local Authority employs the staff, decides on admission arrangements and owns the land and buildings. In foundation schools it is the governing body that has those responsibilities. In foundation and voluntary schools the land is often owned by charitable foundations. Governors' decision-making powers are dependent on the type of school.

(www.peterborough.gov.uk)

As Heads our relationship with the governing body is a crucial one: in effect they are our bosses and are key people with respect to admissions, complaints and disciplinary issues. The Governors have three key roles: providing a strategic view of where the school is heading, acting as a critical friend to the school and holding the school to account for the educational standards it achieves and the quality of education it provides. Governors will also be involved in the process of target setting in line with local and national targets and evaluating progress towards these targets. It is in reality a partnership with the Head and the staff, but Governors should not intervene in the school's day-to-day running. It is not always easy to get this balance right and as Heads we can play an important role in achieving such an appropriate balance.

> Governors should not intervene in the school's day-to-day running

Key tasks for Governors

Working alongside ourselves as Heads, Governors have certain key tasks each term. In the autumn term they must elect a Chair and Vice-Chair, decide on the committee structure, membership and terms of reference, appoint Governors to specific responsibilities, set dates for the year, review results of national tests and agree the staffing structure for the school. Each term they will review the Head's progress towards his or her performance management targets, arrange Governor visits to the school, approve areas of the School Development Plan and School Self-Evaluation, receive a Head of School Report and set up and review pupil performance targets. In the spring term Governors review the pay policy, agree the budget and staffing structure ahead of the new financial year and finalise the School Improvement Plan. Finally, in the summer term, their responsibilities include agreeing the school prospectus and reviewing the attendance of pupils, staff and Governors, pupil exclusions for the year, School Development Plan progress, Head of School Performance with the external advisor and the terms of reference for the Governors.

Officially the governing body should be the author of the development plan. This is often not the case because, whilst the Headteacher will have consulted with staff, it is likely that the Governors are presented with the completed document. This would obviously limit the Governors' strategic role but is often the only practical solution to a difficult and time-consuming process.

For the Governors to have any sense of ownership of the final document they should be in at the start and there should be collaborative planning with the school staff. Governors should also be involved in the monitoring of the plan and its ultimate evaluation against the identified success criteria.

Here are 27 Governor responsibilities:

1. Premises – Health & Safety 2. Budget/Finance/Pay – yearly budget and expenditure 3. Policies 4. Standards of Education 5. Performance Management – Head's Targets 6. Strategic development of the school 7. Appointments – recruitment of staff 8. Critical friend 9. Overall management of the school 10. Determining its aims 11. Monitoring and Evaluating progress 12. Support staff and Head, challenge expectations 13. Monitoring quality of education – learning, attainment 14. Needs of SEN children met 15. School security 16. Sex Education policy 17. Monitoring School Improvement plans and Action Plans 18. Exclusion appeals 19. Admissions 20. Annual report to parents 21. Monitoring visits 22. Holding the school to account 23. Lettings 24. Collective Worship 25. Personnel Issues 26. Monitoring curriculum 27. Complaints

(Taken from Peterborough City Council Governor's Handbook)

The full governing body retains the responsibility for raising standards and giving individual Governors specific curriculum responsibilities can help them monitor the school while ensuring that key curriculum issues remain on the governing body's agenda. It is advisable that schools have nominated Governors for Mathematics, English, SEN, G&T, Child Protection and RE.

brilliant example

Heads can help and advise school Governors in the area of holding the school to account. Ofsted Inspectors will ask to look at Governor minutes to see if Governors are asking the right questions to fulfil this responsibility. As Heads we can ask Governors if they would like support with this aspect of their role and give them examples of the kind of questions they should ask:

● Where have we improved? Do we know why?

● What are the broad trends in the school's achievement in English/ maths compared to similar schools, compared with the national rates of increase and compared with the national picture in terms of gender?

● Are there differences between the achievement of different year groups and if so why?

● How do our results in English/maths compare with those in other subjects?

● What aspects of the subject do pupils find easy/hard?

● Are there significant differences in reading and writing between girls and boys, pupils with special educational needs, very able pupils, pupils with English as an additional language and any other groups e.g. traveller families?

(Taken from Peterborough City Council Governor's Handbook)

Governor visits

Governors should make focused visits to the school so that they can build an effective working relationship with the staff and understand better the context in which they work. As Heads we need to manage this process and agree a policy for this with Governors and staff. Such visits are not about making judgements on the quality of teaching (the Head's responsibility), nor are they about checking on the progress of individual children or pursuing personal agendas. The focus of a visit could be on any policy that is in place in the school, e.g. teaching and learning, marking, assessment, behaviour, collective worship or race equality.

Individual Governors can identify an aspect of the school's work to focus upon which could be a subject, a policy or policies (e.g. behaviour, or a year group). It is better if Governors focus on areas where they have an interest or expertise. The aim will be for them to get to know an aspect of the school really well, and so increase their confidence and knowledge in the process.

Governors could observe:

- *relationships between staff and pupils*
- *relationships between pupils*
- *variety of teaching styles*
- *use of support staff*
- *behaviour and attitude of pupils*
- *enjoyment and enthusiasm*
- *how the pupils are grouped*
- *how different abilities are catered for*
- *children's work*
- *displays*
- *ethos – the atmosphere and values that are evident*
- *use of space and working conditions*
- *quality and quantity of equipment and resources.*

(Taken from Peterborough City Council Governor's Handbook)

Heads report to Governors

There will be at least one full governing body meeting each term for which the Head is required to write a report that will be sent out to all Governors at least two weeks prior to the meeting. The report must cover certain key areas of the school and most Heads' reports will follow a similar format: an introduction commenting briefly upon any special events, concerns or celebrations, and two further sections commenting on pupil and staff issues, successes and achievements. With regard to pupils, exclusions, new statements of special educational need, numbers on the roll, new admissions as well as the results of any appeals for a school place will be covered, and with regard to staff the report will comment on any staff changes, resignations and appointments as well as any changes in responsibilities. Staff attendance, in-service training, including courses attended and performance management updates, should also be included.

The report will also comment on issues to do with standards: results of national tests and exams, findings from any monitoring that has taken place, progress against areas identified by Ofsted, updates on English, Mathematics and ICT (other curriculum areas will be commented upon when something significant has happened). Governors need to be aware of new or revised policies and any Local Authority advisor visits, particularly when the School Improvement Partner has produced a report on the school's progress against the areas covered in the school's self-evaluation. The Governors of course need to be conversant with and have input into the self-evaluation. The Head's report can draw out issues and updates from the self-evaluation to ensure that this involvement is taking place.

the report will also comment on issues to do with standards

The last two areas that must be commented on are buildings/premises issues and financial/budgetary matters. Governors need updating on any major repairs that have taken place, maintenance issues, risk assessments, new builds or alterations, and any health and safety issues including injuries to staff or children. The budget is a fairly straightforward area and will cover an update on the current financial status of the school highlighting any issues, major movements of money from one part of the school budget to another as well as any implications due to admissions or falling numbers of children at the school. Alongside the Head's report is a report from each of the Governor committee groups. The result should be that Governors are updated at the level they need to be on all the relevant school issues that affect the school's development.

A corporate body

The school governing body is a corporate body, which means that it makes decisions and accepts responsibility as a collective. Individual Governors have no powers to act in isolation unless the governing body as a whole delegates responsibility for something to an individual.

The Governors come from different sections of the community and are a diverse group with a range of views and experiences. The categories are there to provide this diversity. (Note that the parent Governors do not represent the parents and do not report back to the parents!) The main responsibility of the governing body is to act as a critical friend that promotes high standards of educational achievement. This will include, amongst many other responsibilities: appointing staff, setting targets for pupil achievement, reviewing staff performance and pay, managing the school budget and ensuring the curriculum is broad and balanced. Following an Ofsted inspection, a Governor's role is critical in terms of ensuring the report is published to parents and the community as well as making sure the action plan is implemented. It is therefore essential that Governors aim to identify problems and tackle them in advance so that when

Ofsted arrives the Governors already have an up-to-date knowledge of the school's strengths and development areas. Governors are appointed for four years and can then be re-elected if they so wish. They can of course resign at any time and can lose their role as a Governor if they fail to attend meetings for a sustained period of time.

Types of Governors

The governing body must be constituted in line with the School Governance Regulations of 2003. These regulations cover the number and type (category) of Governors that make up the governing body. Depending on the category (Community, Foundation, Voluntary Controlled, Voluntary Aided) of the school, the governing body will be made up of different numbers and categories of Governors. In brief, the categories of school Governor are as follows:

- *Parent Governors: selected by election (or appointment if insufficient people stand for election) and drawn from parents and carers of children at the school.*

- *Staff Governors: selected by election from the teaching and support staff who are paid to work at the school.*

- *Community Governors: appointed by the governing body to represent community interests.*

- *Authority Governors – appointed by the LEA.*

- *Foundation Governors (not community schools): appointed by the school's founding body, church or other organisation named in the school's instrument of government.*

- *Partnership Governors (foundation schools only): they replace Foundation Governors if the school does not have a founding body.*

- *Sponsor Governors: discretionary category appointed by the governing body from individuals who have made significant (financial) contributions to the school.*

- *Associate members (not Governors): appointed for their particular skills or experience by the governing body to attend committee meetings and/or full governing body meetings.*

  (Taken from Peterborough City Council Governor Handbook)

Governors may also include representatives from the church, a charitable trust or a business. Special schools sometimes have health authority or voluntary organisation representatives as well.

The governing body must have a Clerk to the Governors, a Chair and a Vice-Chair and can delegate certain responsibilities to individual Governors or certain committees.

A critical friend

Governors should be at the centre of how a school operates, they should be its heartbeat. In this context it is important they make the right decisions and are well informed. In reality this aspiration is challenging for most Governors who strive to get to know the school and fully understand the issues it faces whilst also working in their own full-time jobs, but the degree of efficacy they develop affects the interests of pupils, staff morale and public perception of the school in the same way that the Head does. Governors should support and challenge the Head by questioning and contributing actively to school decision making.

An effective governing body is not there simply to rubber stamp the Head's decision, but in the same way that a school's leadership team must be prepared to give and take and be loyal to collective decisions, so must the governing body as a whole. Governors are protected from any financial liability for the decisions they take as long as they do not break the law.

Heads are keen to attract people to the governing body who can bring energy, experience and fresh ideas. The temptation is to think that very good Governors need to be experts: not so – interest, enthusiasm and commitment are much more important. Ideally we also want Governors to bring a range of experience and interests from many walks of life.

Governors work as a team and this is often something the Head, with the help of experienced Governors, has to remind new governors of (Often parent Governors, in particular, think that their role is to sort out day-to-day issues which are the responsibilities of the Head and the staff – their role is strategic, not operational.) Governors need to focus on whole school strategic issues. Essentially they are responsible for making sure the school provides a good quality education with a focus on raising educational standards. Heads are of course appointed by the Governors – and most Heads choose to be Governors themselves.

Governors need to focus on whole school strategic issues

In summary, both the parent and governing body are significant stakeholders in the school and in the success of the school. The parent body is in effect the customer. Their views are therefore very important and schools should take heed of them and make sure they are aware of them. The governing body leads the school, it does not manage it. It is there to give a long-term strategic direction as to how the school is run and to be a critical friend of the school. In particular, the governing body needs to:

- ensure the school is accountable for its performance to parents and the wider community
- ensure there are plans for the school's future direction
- select the Headteacher
- make decisions on the school's budget and staffing
- make sure the national curriculum is taught
- decide how the school can encourage pupils' spiritual, moral and social development
- make sure the school provides for all its pupils, including those with special needs.

Heads often praise their staff for what they do well but receive little praise themselves and a sometimes overlooked responsibility of Governors is their duty of care towards the Head, ensuring they have an appropriate work–life balance and can manage day-to-day responsibilities effectively. Governors are and should be a true critical friend of the Head.

CHAPTER 7

Self-Evaluation, the SDP, the Budget and Monitoring Standards

n terms of managing a school the four key things that must be in place and linked to each other are the school's own self-evaluation, the School Development Plan (SDP), monitoring and tracking and finally the school budget. The self-evaluation assesses where the school is and prioritises what areas need developing based on the monitoring and tracking data. This informs the SDP and the action points need to be reflected in the budget to ensure the school can afford its priorities and provide good value for money.

Self-evaluation

In addition to all the data analysis a school completes pupils' progress will also be monitored through lesson observations, pupil interviews and book scrutinies. Once the evidence from all these sources is collated then the findings can be submitted to form the school's self-evaluation.

Self-evaluation is best completed by involving as many senior staff as possible. Most schools run a distributed leadership model and so it is important that the people with significant responsibility are contributing to this self-evaluation. The Head is obviously the key person with most significant additional contributions coming from Deputy Heads, senior leaders and key curriculum coordinators. Data on entry is vital information so in primary schools the Foundation Stage Leader needs to be involved and in secondary schools the KS3 (Year 7) Leader must be involved. In addition to this the Special Needs Coordinator will be able to make valuable contributions as will the Gifted and Talented Coordinator.

Self-evaluation is an opportunity to collate in one document all that you do to improve the children's life chances. The completed document can be rewarding reading as it is very impressive to see all this information summarised in one place. Ofsted offers valuable guidance on completing self-evaluation.

Such self-evaluation should not demand long detailed descriptions; it is best described as a brief summary of a school's evaluations and bullet point answers will suffice. It should be concise and follow the bullet points that Ofsted requires comments on, in the order that the document requests them, making it an easier, more accessible document for Ofsted or anyone else to use as a source of information. The completed self-evaluation should be made available for all staff and Governors to read and comment on.

Self-evaluation should comment on and/or grade how effective the school is in up to seven key areas: the school's context, outcomes (how well the pupils are doing), the school's provision, leadership and management, Early Years Foundation Stage, the sixth form and any boarding provision. Part B of the former Ofsted SEF comprises a lot of factual information about the school, staffing, the learners, learners' targets, exclusions, transfers and retention, provision, finance and resources. Part C of the Ofsted SEF is information concerning compliance with statutory requirements or statutory codes of practice and part D focuses on the welfare of boarders and residential pupils where applicable.

Self-evaluation should mirror the evaluation schedule of judgements used by Inspectors so by following it carefully you will be fully prepared to answer Ofsted questions. Ofsted provides grade descriptors to support schools in making judgements and includes key words and statements that serve to ensure you give the correct grade.

brilliant tip

A self-evaluation document is often very detailed and comprehensive so it is advisable to keep it up to date by completing different sections at different times of the year. A school will have its own review cycle so complete your evaluation, section by section, in line with that. Standards, for example, will need to be done once statutory assessment results are available at the end of the summer term or in September.

Ofsted provides guidance called 'The Evaluation Schedule' which is very helpful. The school must grade itself in each section as outstanding, good, satisfactory or inadequate and then justify the grade with evidence statements.

The section on context provides the opportunity to describe the cultural and socio-economic background of the school's catchment, focusing on levels of prosperity or deprivation. Awards such as Healthy Schools, Artsmark or Activemark are recorded in this section.

The section on outcomes asks for comments on the five areas of the former Every Child Matters agenda: pupils' behaviour and the pupils' spiritual, moral, social and cultural development. This is followed by the section on pupils' attainment and the quality of their learning and progress.

Other areas to comment on include attendance, community involvement, pupils' enjoyment of their learning, how safe they feel and to what extent they adopt healthy lifestyles.

A question often asked by Ofsted is what percentage of the teaching in school is good or better and so it is important that the school's assessment of teaching standards is accurate. Another key area is how well the school uses assessment to support learning. The quality of the curriculum and how well it meets children's needs, the effectiveness of the care guidance and support, the engagement with parents and carers as well as the quality of leadership and management including Governors are all graded. The areas of equal opportunities, tackling discrimination, safe-guarding and community cohesion are obviously key areas to comment on and evidence, along with standards and achievement.

> another key area is how well the school uses assessment to support learning

Finally the school's self-evaluation, in line with Ofsted Inspectors' judgements, should comment on the school's capacity for sustained improvement and whether the school provides good value for money. These are key parts of the overall effectiveness judgement. One way to substantiate grades is in discussion with the SIP whose brief includes agreeing self-evaluation grades. These views and comments from the SIP report can then be included to support self-evaluation judgements.

The School Development Plan

The School Development Plan is the second key document in school that should be informed by the findings of a school's monitoring cycle and then fed into the self-evaluation document. Different from the self-evaluation its focus is setting objectives to move the school forward ensuring that its infrastructure, equipment and educational provision are up to date and fit for purpose and, most importantly, reflect the needs of the pupils. The effectiveness of the SDP is dependent upon financial resources being available to support the objectives that it sets out to achieve.

SDP objectives need to be SMART (Specific, measurable, achievable, realistic and timed). The school as a whole needs to own the objectives and there should be clear responsibility and accountability for their implementation, monitoring and success criteria. Heads can list main priorities for their school's continued improvement from the SDP and the self-evaluation also demands identification of such priorities. As time passes objectives are achieved and ultimately embedded in the school's practice so priorities naturally change.

If finances or time precludes objectives being achieved then the Head must, in conjunction with staff and Governors, agree to scale down the objectives so that they are realistically achievable and affordable. It is a natural trait of leaders to want the best and initially we must not be surprised if our plans turn out to be too ambitious!

School development must be realistic. Each subject coordinator will want to develop their area of the curriculum and may request the resources they believe are necessary to do this. It is the Head's, Governors' and Leadership Teams' responsibility to prioritise at a whole school strategic level, and the Head's response to resource requests should be based upon the identified school priorities.

brilliant case study

The School Development Plan contains the school aims and vision statement that developments should be in line with and it also contains a list of the main school priorities. The Development Plan has grown out of the school's self-evaluation framework. It seeks to build on and continue the successful work of previous years and address identified areas with scope for further improvement. Starting with the school aims, which are often complementary to the Every Child Matters agenda, it seeks to set out a vision and the steps required for achieving this vision. It is, however, a working document that evolves and develops. Governors and senior staff are directly involved in drawing up the key issues and all staff are consulted. The Leadership Team develop and prioritise the key issues from this plan, which bases itself in the findings of the school's Ofsted monitoring and therefore the contents of the self-evaluation. Each member of staff has a curriculum responsibility and is part of a curriculum team that is responsible for completing and updating its section of the school development plan.

Curriculum Coordinators and/or Team Leaders create a development plan that reflects the priorities of the school's self-evaluation and responds to the monitoring and evaluation findings that are on-going throughout each school year. Curriculum and Phase Team Leaders monitor learning and teaching throughout the school and report their findings to the Deputy Heads verbally and in writing. The key messages are then reported to the Head by Deputy Heads and Phase Team Leaders. The Head completes their own report to summarise the resulting school priorities. All of this informs the self-evaluation and is reported to School Governors. The Head and Deputies check the findings through staff review meetings, analysis of data, pupil interviews, work scrutinies and joint observations with curriculum and Phase Team Leaders.

The budget

One of the biggest concerns when taking on headship is often the running of a budget. The size of each budget depends on the size of the school as funding is calculated by an agreed sum of money per pupil. This amount may vary from one Local Authority to another and from one educational sector to another with secondary age children often getting more money per head than those at primary age. Special schools usually get an even greater sum per head.

Place funding also varies per child for infant-aged children, junior-aged children and nursery-aged children. This is called the formula funding or the AWPU (age weighted pupil unit). This is the first issue to look at when seeking to understand a school's income derivation.

Special needs funding

Every school will get a sum of money for special educational needs (SEN) and possibly also for medical hours to pay for staff responsible for SEN (like the SENCo (Special Needs Coordinator) and the LST (Learning Support Teacher)) as well as any staff who work with statemented children or children with medical conditions. A child gets a statement because they have a very high level of need. The child may, for example, suffer from Down's syndrome or autism, have global delay or have significant behaviour problems. About 2–3% of the school population have a statement so they tend to be very high-level need and require one-to-one support. The SEN budget is designed to pay for a Learning Support Assistant (LSA) to work with each statemented child as and when support is needed.

Standards Fund Grants

One of the largest sums of money to come into the budget has historically been the Standards Fund Grants. These grants were unpredictable as they were only guaranteed on a year-to-year or limited period basis, so you could not guarantee that a grant you got one year under this heading would be there the following year. Some of these grants were for specific projects such as ICT equipment or improving staffing facilities. About two-thirds of the budget comes from the AWPU and the rest from a variety of grants as well as money collected from parents and carers to support educational visits etc.

Many of the former Standards Fund Grants were concerned with standards-raising initiatives that are introduced to try and improve test results and they were often ring-fenced for use with the affected cohort. There are initiatives for other year groups but generally they are aimed at trying to raise attainment in national tests in the short term. There have also been grants to support PE initiatives as obviously health and fitness issues are politically expedient. Grants can be given to support paying for in-service training and supply teachers whilst staff are out on training. In 2010 the new government introduced the Pupil Premium to replace some of the former Standards Fund Grants.

Capital Fund Grant

Another significant sum of money that schools receive is the Capital Fund for school building improvement. This fund is spent in line with the school's asset management plan that identifies, in priority order, what building improvements are needed. In older schools it may be replacing windows, resurfacing flat roofs, upgrading the heating system and electrics or resurfacing outside areas.

It is very hard to accurately assess how much money will be in a budget at the start of the budget building process in February and supplementary grants may be devolved into the budget throughout the year: as Heads we cannot always predict the amount we will receive and its allocated purpose. Extra funding is received if the school has a swimming pool on site and also following the appointment of any Newly Qualified Teachers. Historically there have also been grants to do with the level of free school meals, social deprivation and prior attainment based on pupil attainment levels. This list is not exhaustive and may vary from one local authority to another. However once all these grants have been included in a budget we have the grand total that is the school's formula budget allocation.

Balancing the budget

Between 80% and 85% of a school's budget is spent on staffing! The higher the percentage is above 80% the more likely savings will have to be made, for example through redundancy. Staffing obviously includes teaching staff, support staff, office staff, cleaners and catering (unless you buy into a service) and supply staff. (Some schools have Higher Level Teaching Assistants or Cover Supervisors instead of supply teachers. There will then be staff development costs and staff related insurance to cater for.)

Schools pay into a number of services including grounds maintenance, personnel services, Governor Services and building maintenance services. On top of this the school must pay rates, phone bills, water and gas, electricity and/or oil. Annually the electrical and gas appliances and the fire equipment need checking and in some cases replacing.

After budgeting for services and running costs budgets for phases of school, departments, curriculum areas and administration costs are addressed. ICT equipment is a significant cost encompassing equipment, running costs and a broadband connection. Photocopiers are universally used and can be expensive.

Other issues that have to be planned for include replacing carpets, blinds and curtains as well as painting the building and that may all need to be done on a rolling programme. Certain curriculum areas need equipment that can be very expensive, PE equipment needs maintaining and inspecting for safety as do outdoor play areas, pianos need tuning and broken, lost and outdated equipment needs replacing.

> certain curriculum areas need equipment that can be very expensive

Building the budget is not a difficult task; prioritising may be harder, but really there are comparatively small amounts of money that we have any degree of flexibility over.

Financial Management Standard in Schools (FMSiS)

FMSiS was introduced in October 2006 and in January 2007 schools, legally, had to meet those standards. Proving that the school has met the standards requires collecting evidence. The standards help schools evaluate how well they are managing the school finances and an added bonus is that they provide a very good checklist which helps train Finance Secretaries and Bursars in recognised good practice so that they improve. FMSiS does not introduce higher standards or anything new for the school to do but simply helps the school assess how well they are doing against what they should be doing anyway.

FMSiS sets out its requirements to be assessed in five areas:

1 Leadership and Governance.

2 People Management.

3 Policy and Strategy.

4 Partnerships and Resources.

5 Processes.

In 2010 the government removed the need to meet the FMSiS standards but it still remains a very good benchmarking tool.

Monitoring standards

Assessment and data are central to a school's perceived success. The ability to prove that what we are doing is effective is absolutely key in terms of accountability and judgements about the school. Figure 7.1 is a simple model that attempts to encapsulate what assessment and data aims to inform.

Standards and progress are what a school essentially focuses on in terms of accountability; comparisons with national statistics and progress from the end of one key stage to the end of the next are key factors. How much progress is each class and each year group making annually? Obviously at primary level this is

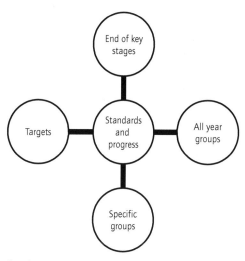

Figure 7.1 Simple assessment and data model

all focused on English and Mathematics but the principles are the same when applied to any subject area.

At KS1, the main focus is Reading, Writing, Speaking and Listening, Mathematics and Science and at KS2 it is Reading, Writing and Mathematics. At KS3 and KS4 each subject area is accountable for the progress that is made and the standards that are achieved. However it is fair to say that the greatest emphasis is put upon the English and Mathematics results that our schools attain.

Standards

Standards is all about how we compare to all schools nationally and to schools that are in a similar situation socially and culturally (known as our statistical neighbours). The focus is on the percentage of children achieving the expected level and the higher level, and in more depth the percentages of children achieving the expected mini level or fine grade progress. At KS1 the expectation is to reach Level 2b and at KS2 Level 4b. At KS4, the expectation is that pupils will achieve five 'A*' to 'C' grades including English and Mathematics.

SATs results are converted into points scores in order to calculate the average points scores for a school cohort. Figure 7.2 illustrates how national curriculum levels are converted into points to enable calculation of an average points score.

KS1 conversions

P1-3	P4-6	P7.8	1c	1b	1a	2c	**2b**	2a	3c	3b
1	3	5	7	9	11	13	**15**	17	19	21

KS2 conversions

3c	3b	3a	4c	**4b**	4a	5c	5b
19	21	23	25	**27**	31	33	35

Figure 7.2 Average points scores

At any Key Stage schools aim for two outcomes: firstly that the average points score is equal to or above the expectation (15 at KS1 and 27 at KS2) and secondly that it demonstrates a year-on-year improvement for the school.

brilliant tip

If the average points score for one year is not as good as the previous cohort's then collate the average points scores for the last three to five years, whatever works to your advantage as a school. Hopefully this will demonstrate that the school is doing well over a period of time and the current cohort's results are simply a blip not a downward trend.

Comparison with previous years is key as the Local Authority and Ofsted will look at trends over time. The ideal is to have three consecutive years of improving results. The comparison with predictions, targets and results must be analysed as the expectation is that we have such robust systems that we can predict accurately and meet challenging yet realistic targets that have been agreed with our school Governors and the Local Authority.

Targeting focus groups

Within tracking systems schools should be able to analyse specific groups' performance, comparing them with previous years and predictions/targets. Groups may alter according to school contexts but generally we look at the performance of the following groups: all pupils, boys/girls, and White British compared to EAL (English as an Additional Language) pupils (e.g. Pakistani heritage, Eastern Europeans and Afro-Caribbean). Progress of SEN groups must be tracked as well as the progress of Looked After Children, those who are eligible for free school meals (FSM) and Able, Gifted or Talented pupils. In-depth group analysis provides schools with evidence to allocate group intervention initiatives.

brilliant tip

Analyse the pupils who have been at your school for the whole of the key stage. Hopefully this will illustrate that if a pupil stays at your school over a long period of time they progress well. If you have intervention programmes in place, for example for vulnerable pupils, then track their progress. With any luck this will illustrate the good progress they are making as a result of the intervention.

It is worth tracking the progress of likely underperforming groups (e.g. persistent absentees and newly arrived children that come with no English as well as those children who have emotional and behavioural problems). What do the results look like when certain groups, including statemented children, are removed?

National average progress is one full National Curriculum level every two years or six mini-levels every two years. Under this guidance we can now check on the percentage of children who make three mini-levels between Y2 and Y4 for example. The aim is to keep children on track for their predicted level in Year 6 based on their Year 2 assessment or on track for a particular grade at GCSE based on their attainment on entry in Year 7.

With the class teacher or tutor it is important to refine all pupils' targets annually, taking into account SEN levels, vulnerability and language issues. Always bear in mind, however, the overall percentage targets for each cohort at the end of the key stage.

It is important to be very alert to children who miss their targets over two consecutive years – they can severely damage the schools Contextual Value Added (CVA) scores and those pupils will then need targeted intervention such as one-to-one tuition to catch up.

Useful documents to refer to, to help with this area of data analysis are:

- the school's RAISE report that highlights historical comparisons of attainment, average points and CVA
- any Local Authority School Profiles that give detailed analysis of SATs results at the different key stages including analysis of groups, historical trends and comparisons with local and national standards
- Fischer Family Trust reports: these provide targets for individual children and individual cohorts taking into account gender, month of birth, postcode (re deprivation index) and previous key stage attainment.

 **brilliant** recap

Schools must have robust monitoring systems but it is essential to approach all this data with a healthy dose of common sense and remember that children are young people with their own lives to lead, their own personalities and priorities, and not robots that will automatically progress at the expected mini-level development rate because that is what the statisticians and politicians want! They simply may not be interested or they may be the next Sir Richard Branson, Delia Smith, Simon Cowell, David Beckham, John Lennon, Duncan Ballentyne, Lord Alan Sugar or Sir Michael Parkinson. None of them did exceptionally well at school or went to university and life seems to have treated them well in terms of success!

CHAPTER 8

A diverse job

n this chapter we will look at the main areas of responsibility and ways of working that come together to form the day-to-day workload of a Head. Such areas include initiating change, communication, personnel management, the pupil voice, assessment and testing, policies, health and safety, safe-guarding, the work–life balance, Every Child Matters and public relations.

Rebel with a cause

One Head's advice to me when I first started as a new Head was to bin most of the paperwork that arrived on my desk as he believed anything of importance would be re-sent! I can see the logic but have never followed that advice as in this ecologically friendly world it would not be a very 'green' thing to do. Since then technology has taken over and most things get sent by e-mail: if I neglect my e-mails for a few days I come back to the equivalent of a post office van full of letters! The majority of them find the computer's recycle bin as opposed to the paper bin so perhaps in a modern day context that Head's original advice is sound.

There have been some initiatives thrust upon schools that could have been ignored and often as long as a school can show that what it offers is good and effective then you can ignore a great deal of what is seemingly being imposed. Conversely, it is possible to introduce initiatives into schools from the grass roots but you can encounter obstacles when taking this approach.

On two occasions when I introduced new initiatives independently of the Local Authority other schools joined in – I enjoyed being a rebel! One initiative involved introducing a very effective way to teach reading with the consequence that all the local authority training on reading became irrelevant. I introduced creativity and creative curriculum approaches into school long before they became nationally popular and over half the schools in the Local Authority initially signed up to participate in the work. Once again the initiative came from the schools rather than from advisors or government. I could sense resistance from Inspectors and Advisors but as I have already stated, you are in a powerful position as a Head when it comes to taking a decisive lead. Creativity became a government mantra and suddenly I became a beacon of good practice although losing the 'rebel with a cause' tag made life less exciting!

Heads must realise that they are in a powerful position and can make significant decisions about what initiatives their school will adopt as there are very few educational reforms that are enshrined in law.

Realising that Local Authorities and advisors are there to serve not to dictate allows Heads to be selective and not say yes to everything that is thrust upon them by government.

Communication

Heads have a huge volume of mail to read. Ofsted and the government love e-mail – they made a decision to reduce the amount and frequency of paperwork sent to schools then started to e-mail everything so it is not classified as paperwork and they can send it in bulk!

Of course there are also a huge number of meetings! School Governor meetings are essential and they add up to a significant number with often two Full Governor meetings a term, usually in the evening, then termly Governor committee meetings on premises, finance, personnel, curriculum and, less frequently, admissions. There are staff meetings, leadership meetings, department meetings, staff briefings and meetings to arrange meetings! In addition to this as Heads we are often involved in Local Authority Heads meetings once or twice a term as well as half termly cluster Heads meetings with the schools in our vicinity. In addition to this Heads may well be involved in a local authority strategy group on finance, curriculum, admissions or schools forums. As well as all of these there are the courses and conferences run by private providers that Heads attend out of choice for personal development: Ofsted, the National College and the NAHT, for example, run exceptionally good training events and personally I would not miss the National College annual conference as it is so inspirational.

There are meetings tailored to your own school with the Local Authority Advisor and the School Improvement Partner. Our school has the status of being a National School of Creativity which brings with it meetings in London and Newcastle as well as other events all round the country and many schools may be involved in something equivalent. In addition to all of this many Heads will be involved in social services and child protection meetings. I am sure I will have missed something in this long list! There is no escaping the fact that headship does entail its fair share of meetings, form filling, e-mail responses, box-ticking and data analysis as well.

> headship does entail its fair share of meetings

Performance management, in-service training and lesson observations

All schools must have a performance management (PM) policy, often produced by the school's personnel advisors (EPM in my case) that are available to all staff, and Local Authorities (Peterborough for our school) usually deliver training. I have used these two sources to ensure the details below are correct. It is important that all staff in a school have a performance management review that is done fairly and consistently across the school. Assessment for passing through the threshold onto the upper pay spine is now also done through the performance management cycle.

A Performance Management Reviewer is chosen by the Headteacher and trained in observation. The Reviewer has all tasks delegated by the Headteacher and is responsible for support, observations, planning statement and pay progression for eligible staff. Eligible staff are Advanced Skills Teachers, those on the leadership scale, or through the threshold, all main scale teachers as well as support and administrative staff. Newly Qualified Teachers in their first year of teaching are not part of the cycle as they have their own monitoring cycle and targets to cover in order to pass and qualify as a teacher. All staff automatically receive a pay increment unless they are subject to capability procedures due to under-performance. Heads, Deputy/Assistant Heads and threshold staff must achieve their identified targets to progress to the next pay level. Unqualified teachers are also a part of this cycle due to their pay scale. Higher Level Teaching Assistants may also be used to review the performance of other support staff, as long as it is part of their job description.

It is recommended that at least one hour is scheduled at least five working days in advance of when the performance management meeting takes place. In the review meeting the previous year's objectives must be reviewed and arrangements for any observations to take place should be agreed as well as training, development and support that are to be provided. Timescales at which the objectives are to be achieved are agreed and whilst these need not be constrained to one year, some annual milestones need to be in place. The member of staff's job description must be agreed and signed and any pay progression, if appropriate, agreed before the end of the meeting.

When agreeing a member of staff's objectives relevant professional standards or whole school/team objectives identified in the School Development Plan will be integrated as well as pupil progress targets. In addition to this it is important to cater for an individual's professional aspirations as well as giving due consideration to their work–life balance. Objectives must be challenging but achievable. Success criteria must also be clear so that staff are aware of how they are to be judged. If a member of staff wishes to progress onto the UPS (Upper Pay Scale) levels then these standards should be considered and integrated into their performance management targets. UPS is now part of and must be integrated into the PM cycle with decisions being made by the PM Reviewer.

All aspects of the performance management cycle should be planned at the initial meeting. Observations will be agreed and the recommendation is that observations should not exceed a maximum of three hours a year, excluding Ofsted, HMI, Local Authority Inspections, School Improvement Advisor and agreed drop-ins. Although unions recommend a maximum of three hours of observations a year there is no statutory restriction on the number of hours a teacher can be observed. Each school should have a policy that is agreed with staff about how many observations will be undertaken in a year.

brilliant example

The school I work in, with the agreement of staff, has two senior staff observing a lesson so that teaching and learning as well as a particular curriculum focus can be observed at the same time. The advantage of this is that the two senior staff can discuss and agree how well the lesson went and what grade it should be given. This approach leads to valuable professional dialogue between the senior staff and the feedback that the teacher receives is then substantiated by two people and is, therefore, reassuringly more accurate from everyone's point of view.

Only trained members of staff who have observed alongside senior staff to learn about the protocols of such monitoring should give feedback. Once again guidelines should be provided for staff and agreed by staff so that there is an expectation of how all involved will behave. As Headteachers we must adopt a protocol for classroom observation within our performance management policy.

brilliant tip

When observing a lesson it is important that the member of staff being observed is relaxed so when the observer enters they should smile and greet the teacher warmly, setting a supportive and friendly tone from the outset. Another good strategy is to take up a place in the classroom out of the direct vision of the teacher; after all it is the children's reaction and engagement that the observer is most interested in.

There should be an agreed focus for a lesson observation and the observer should avoid intervening during the lesson unless it is a dangerous situation. Equally they should not correct any teacher errors in front of the pupils but make a note of them and feed them back in a sensitive way at a later date. Finally, as the observer leaves the lesson they should smile, thank the teacher and arrange a time for feedback allowing both parties to have time to reflect. Officially feedback must be given within five days.

Only the named reviewer is able to observe a performance management observation, although other coordinators can if it links with the SDP. Peer observations are also good practice as long as this is agreed beforehand and is not part of the performance management cycle.

It may in certain circumstances be that provision and change to objectives may be necessary due to illness, a change of year group or responsibility, and if this happens the PM reviewer must follow the standard regulation process. Professional dialogue should continue through the year in support of the objectives to monitor progress. Evidence of progress should be shared when it becomes available and either party can request a meeting to discuss performance management issues.

If objectives are not being met, the performance management cycle is removed and capability procedures are put in place, personnel are informed and pay increases can end if there is evidence that shows a lack of progress over a significant period of time. The same reviewer will see the whole cycle through unless a teacher leaves or circumstances change within a school to warrant a change and under such circumstances information should be handed over.

Heads may only intervene in someone's performance management if it is felt that the planning statement is not consistent with other statements, or the PM policy. Heads must also have performance management targets and usually two or three Governors will be appointed to review the Head's objectives that are set with these Governors and an outside advisor or the School Improvement Partner.

CPD (continual professional development) for each member of staff can be integrated into their performance management objectives. Teachers should play an active role in their own CPD and the reviewer should be active in supporting their choices. CPD is the way that teachers can maintain, improve and broaden their knowledge and ability and so develop the skills they need to improve their professional performance. CPD can take several forms: it can be organised within school using your own school's expertise or it can be external courses arranged by the Local Authority, FE colleges, universities, subject associations or private providers. Networks of schools can get together to organise joint events and of course each school will have its own staff meeting programme and professional day agendas. Good quality CPD, or life-long learning, has a significant impact on a member of staff's personal development and consequently a positive impact on the quality of a child's education. All teachers should have access to high-quality training and development opportunities throughout their career.

> teachers should play an active role in their own CPD

The pupil voice

Effective use of the pupil voice can have a very positive impact on a school in terms of school improvement and pupils playing an active part in the life and decision-making processes of the school. The idea is to make pupils legitimate partners in the school change/decision-making processes so that they are active partners in their own education rather than simply its recipients.

The obvious starting point is having a school council and some schools allocate them a budget and real decision-making powers so that they are genuinely consulted about their views on their school. It is essential that the school council has some power in order to gain the respect and support of other pupils. In some schools pupils have been involved in staff interviews and even in budget-building decisions. It is common for pupils to be involved in lesson planning with staff including commenting on their own individual learning to address the personalised learning agenda. Other roles for pupils in schools may include being house captains, language assistants (who translate for and support newly arrived children from other parts of the world) or as in our school 'mini-creative agents' that support our curriculum development.

Pupils can also be involved in School Development Plans, surveys, teaching and learning, behaviour management strategies, ICT issues, reviews of induction procedures, pupil voice conferences and supervising lunchtime activities. Issues that pupils may be consulted upon could also include school meals, the healthy schools agenda, graffiti and vandalism issues, the school environment and school uniform. The more involved they are in the school and the more decision-making powers they are allowed, the greater their feeling of ownership for the school, which will naturally have a positive impact on their behaviour, attendance and learning.

brilliant example

As part of a group of schools called Oasis that networked within Peterborough to look at a creative curriculum approach, the manager, Di Goldsmith, created student consultant groups from each of the schools that wished to be involved. They visited each other's schools to discuss learning and learning activities as well as participating in some creative learning experiences. This followed on from the QCA residential conference, 'What Makes Learning Worth It?', that Oasis organised with QCA for children from all over the country. Teachers learnt a great deal about what makes learning 'worth it' and how children learn best. At the QCA conference, when asked what makes learning worth it one pupil replied, 'I can't explain it but it is something from your own heart, something that inspires you.' I think she could be right!

Through the pupil voice we can also support pupils to become actively involved in the life of not only their school but also the wider community where they can address both social and cultural issues. Pupils will then develop the skills of enquiry, negotiation and communication. In our effort to make children independent learners, responsible citizens and confident individuals the exploration of social and cultural issues develops their decision-making skills, which will hopefully lead to them taking responsible actions and being involved in society in a positive way.

Assessment and testing: AfL and APP

Heads are obliged to ensure that formal summative assessments take place at the end of each key stage except KS3. Most Headteachers have no problem with such testing; where there is controversy is in the way the tests are reported and used to judge schools. Rather than dwell on these tests let us look at what other forms of assessment exist and what merits they may have. I will focus on two key initiatives.

Heads continually look to implement best practice across a school and two initiatives that seem to have had a very positive impact on children's learning are Assessment for Learning (AfL) and Assessing Pupils' Progress (APP). The two initiatives work alongside each other to give a greater understanding for pupils of their next steps in learning, encouraging them to be leaders of their own learning. AfL involves staff and pupils discussing and evaluating the effectiveness of the pupils' work and agreeing appropriate feedback that will inform the next steps in learning. These discussions should help build teachers' confidence in their own judgements and support them in their future planning. Assessment for learning encourages discussion about where a learner is in their learning, and where they are aiming to be. This is achieved by sharing learning objectives with the pupils, agreeing the next steps in their learning, developing success criteria together, and engaging throughout the lesson in effective questioning and feedback so that learning can be modified to suit pupils' individual needs. Good practice in AfL involves children recapping on previous learning, introduction of the learning objective, exploring the children's own ideas and prior knowledge, continual reference to the agreed success criteria for the lesson, consistent feedback to the pupils, self- and peer assessment during the lesson, reflection on the learning throughout with a final plenary at the end of the lesson when the learning that has taken place is discussed and developed with a recap of the learning that has taken place.

the two initiatives work alongside each other

brilliant tip

The Scottish Learning and Teaching website states that learners learn best when they: understand clearly what they are trying to learn, and what is expected of them; when they are given feedback about the quality of their work and what they can do to make it better; when they are given advice about how to go about making improvements; and finally when they are fully involved in deciding what needs to be done next, and who can give them help if they need it.

APP is a structured approach to school assessment and complements the AfL approach. It focuses on pupils' attainment rather than being an ongoing day-to-day assessment tool in the way that AfL is. It matches up to national standards and National Curriculum levels. It is a great support to staff as it develops their understanding of progression from one national curriculum level to another. As such it provides information about the strengths and areas of development of individual pupils and groups of pupils providing the teachers with information highlighting which children need to be targeted for extra support. In addition to this APP informs curriculum planning and ensures that teaching is matched to pupils' needs.

There are two main issues with non-test-based assessment and that is getting a level of consistency from one teacher to another and one school to another, and despite schools participating in a wide range of moderating exercises this is still hard to achieve. The other issue is that of workload: APP in particular has been criticised for the significant amount of time it takes teachers to effectively implement.

However, accurate on-going assessment procedures that inform planning, learning and teaching and a tracking facility like APP that measures the standards children are attaining are essential tools in a school for a Head that wants to monitor and assess progress in a school and be accountable.

Policies, safeguarding and health and safety

As Heads we must ensure that all safeguarding and health and safety procedures are in place and reviewed on a regular agreed basis. Governors have a responsibility for this as well. Certain policies need reviewing on an annual basis and personnel advisors to the school will produce updated policies that schools can adopt. This is essential especially when there are issues like redundancy and complaints. Policies must be agreed and reviewed by the school governing body and it is advisable to consult with staff on certain policies before they are implemented.

Safeguarding is a key area for all Heads; it is not just about protecting children from deliberate harm, as Ofsted highlight, it includes issues for schools such as pupil health and safety, bullying, racist abuse, harassment and discrimination, use of physical intervention, meeting the needs of pupils with medical conditions, providing first aid, drug and substance misuse, educational visits, intimate care, internet safety and issues which may be specific to a local area or population (e.g. gang activity and school security). Schools must also have a very thorough system for recording the details of staff appointments and CRB checks.

brilliant example

This shows the headings that are needed on a school record to ensure that staff have been vetted correctly:

Identity				Qualifications	
Name	Address	Date of birth	Evidenced, date, by whom	Qualifications required: yes/ no	Qualifications required: evidenced, date, by whom
Overseas checks		**List 99**	**CRB**	**Right to work in UK**	
Checks required: yes/no	Checks carried out: yes/no	Check, evidenced, date, by whom	Check, evidenced, date, by whom	Check, evidenced and date	

When self-evaluating, Ofsted guidance requires that the following key questions need asking with regard to safeguarding:

- How safe do pupils feel in school, including their understanding of issues relating to safety, such as bullying?
- To what extent do pupils feel able to seek support from the school should they feel unsafe?
- What are the pupils' own views about being safe and free from harassment?

Work–life balance

This is an important area in terms of school workforce development. As Heads we should appreciate that everyone's work–life balance is different: some staff immerse themselves in their work and school becomes their life but this would not suit others. The national agreement states that all teachers, including Headteachers, should enjoy a reasonable work–life balance. It goes on to describe this balance as being 'about helping teachers combine work with their personal interests outside work'. Teaching is obviously one of the 'caring' professions and it is often not easy to leave the job behind as children's needs so often remain on your mind in your desire to support and help them to achieve their best. In addition to this, planning, preparation, assessment and marking can be very time-consuming.

It is a Head's responsibility to ensure that teachers' workload is not too much of a burden, but many teachers will do more from choice as they strive to do their best for the children. Planning, preparation and assessment (PPA) time, which guarantees that 10% of their working week is release time from the classroom, has helped to reduce the burden but has brought with it an administrative challenge for Heads and senior leaders as we strive to ensure that this time out of the classroom is suitably covered. Senior staff who are heavily involved in leadership and monitoring roles will need additional release time to carry out their duties and Newly Qualified Teachers are entitled to a total of 20% of their timetable to be non-contact. As part of the government's agenda to provide a better work–life balance, part of the workforce agreement identifies certain jobs that support and administrative staff should do rather than teachers. Once again as Heads we should ensure that this is taking place and that this is clearly stated in job descriptions. There should also be policies to clarify how often a teacher can be expected to cover for absent colleagues and how Teaching Assistants, Cover Supervisors and Higher Level Teaching Assistants are used to cover the absence of a teacher. Heads must ensure transparency in all aspects of release and cover arrangements.

> ensure that teachers' workload is not too much of a burden

Benefits of a reasonable work–life balance should include reduced sickness and stress levels and improved emotional well-being so that staff morale is higher and their motivation increased. Sometimes staff need support with time management: for example some staff take a lot longer to complete planning than others. Ideally a good work–life balance should lead to improved learning for the pupils and a greater level of efficiency.

If open and honest relationships exist in a school alongside good communication then hopefully there is increased job satisfaction and in the end there will be a positive impact on the children's education, which is the focus of all we do in schools. All staff, like all children, are different and to get the best out of staff we as Heads need to differentiate in the way they deal with individuals. It is an area that as Heads we must strive to get right if the school is to be successful, but it is a tall order to keep all staff happy and content at all times!

Every Child Matters (ECM)

This was a key and very important document upon which schools were judged at Ofsted inspections and sections of the SEF invite you to comment upon each area. The five areas, or outcomes as they are referred to, are:

1. Be Healthy
2. Stay Safe

3. Enjoy and Achieve

4. Make a Positive Contribution

5. Achieve Economic Well-being.

ECM was renamed 'Helping Children Achieve More' in 2010.

Between them the outcomes cover physical health, mental and emotional health, sexual health, healthy lifestyles, drug use, bullying, discrimination, anti-social behaviour, standards in education, enjoyment of school, being law abiding, developing positive relations, developing enterprising behaviour and being prepared for further education and/or employment. QCDA summed it up well by saying that we want pupils to be successful learners, confident individuals and responsible citizens.

ECM is likely to form the foundations of a school but all too often it seems that the main focus by which all of these key issues are measured is how well pupils perform in SATs and examinations. ECM has many comparisons to Maslow's hierarchy of needs, for unless children are safe, have a good diet, a comfortable place to sleep and are loved they are unlikely to succeed in life.

brilliant case study

A learning walk around a small, rural primary school one afternoon revealed the extent to which ECM is embedded in every aspect of the school. Overtly there were posters encouraging children to wash their hands, eat a balanced diet and come to after-school 'Stay and Swim' (Be Healthy), and pupils in upper KS2 were rehearsing their end of year play 'The Bully' (Stay Safe). More subtly I observed the Headteacher's Assistant (a Year 6 pupil) meet with the Head to discuss how she would like to spend her wages: pupils apply for jobs in the school and given that they fulfil their duties over a period of time they are paid in tokens that can be exchanged for stationery and games out of a school catalogue (Achieve Economic Well-being). Outside

Reception children were completing sponsored laps of the school field raising money for a worthy local cause (Make a Positive Contribution) whilst in the KS1 classroom children were thoroughly absorbed in preparing their individual roles in a forthcoming mock wedding with unparalleled fervour (Enjoy and Achieve). It was clear that in this school Every Child Matters is part of every aspect of the curriculum and enrichment life of the school.

Public relations

Historically schools have never really had to consider public relations but in recent years there has been a need to promote our schools, particularly in the secondary sector where there can be fierce competition for school places. School websites are now quite elaborate and a lot of thought is given to school entrances to make them attractive and welcoming. First impressions are always important and it is key that the voice on the phone or the person at the front desk is warm, welcoming and smiling!

However one of the most significant visual factors for a school is the front entrance and foyer. Visual messages are as important as oral messages and Heads must ensure that schools are well promoted in every way.

brilliant example

The entrance foyer and office area are large and welcoming as well as being secure. Automatic doors slide away to allow the visitor to enter a large entrance foyer with comfortable settees to sit on and a large TV screen displaying information about the school including photographs from school lessons, events and trips. In front of you is a large welcoming desk area with computer/internet access available, plaques denoting the school's achievements displayed prominently and happy welcoming office staff to greet you. The entrance gives a loud and clear message about the school.

Staff throughout the school should make visitors and parents/ carers welcome – the children and their families are after all our customers and should be treated with respect.

The danger as in all walks of life is that public relations are seen as something that is needed when something goes wrong. More often that not it is the Head that takes on the role of the PR person. Public relations should of course be proactive and preventative and so a lot of it is about how the school communicates with its community. Some schools have an open-door policy where parents are welcomed into school in the mornings and have a chance to speak to staff, which can result in potential issues being dealt with early on. As Sir Tim Brighouse explains the key to successful public relations is to try to influence the way the community perceives the school and as Heads we should take every opportunity at sports days, open evenings and other school events to promote our schools. It is important to ensure that all the good things about the school are what the community perceives the school to be about and we need to plan this and not leave it to chance.

 **brilliant** recap

What a job headship is: exciting, unpredictable, all-consuming, hectic, diverse, challenging… and so on and so on. What I hope to have achieved in this chapter is to give an outline of what the job entails and then focus on the key areas of headship, the ones you have to get right to ensure that the school will run smoothly so that the pupils get the best possible deal that they can.

What this chapter highlights more than anything is how diverse the Head's job is. In the primary sector more than the secondary, due to the size of the schools, there are often less levels of management to deal with issues under a distributed leadership model. In Chapter 6 I dealt with leadership issues and the importance of the distributed leadership model. This chapter goes some way to describing why leadership in a school can no longer be a one-person job.

The essential message to take away is how all the key areas of the job must link together in the common purpose of school improvement aimed at enhancing the school's provision for children and young adults.

CHAPTER 9

Ofsted

This chapter aims to address the worries and concerns many Heads feel when facing an external inspection. Whilst clarifying the reality of an inspection and the considerable level of accountability that Heads hold, it also explores actions that can be taken across an academic year to ensure that when 'the call' comes each individual will feel confident and prepared. The chapter is divided into three main areas: an overview of Ofsted and its effectiveness; my experiences of Ofsted; and finally a more objective, advice-based approach to preparing for Ofsted. I have used the very informative and helpful Ofsted website to ensure advice and facts are correct.

Ofsted: Raising Standards, Improving Lives

Ofsted is the Office for Standards in Education, Children's Services and Skills. Ofsted describes its role as 'to regulate and inspect to achieve excellence in the care of children and young people, and in education and skills for learners of all ages'. These aims and their purpose are entirely appropriate as it simply wishes to raise aspirations and help ensure better life chances for children no matter what their background or circumstances. Ofsted is not linked to the government but to parliament and in that way can claim to be impartial with respect to party politics. My experience is that this is true, insofar as it will make an appropriate judgement, irrespective of whether the school is following government initiatives or not. As long as a school is raising standards of achievement then Ofsted will support and sanction it.

The Education and Inspections Act, which established Ofsted, specifically requires that it simply:

- promote service improvement
- ensure services focus on the interests of their users
- see that services are efficient, effective and promote value for money.

The Ofsted brief is wide; it inspects early years and childcare, children's social care, schools, colleges, initial teacher training, Support Services, adult education and more! Ofsted assesses children's services in local areas, and inspects services for looked after children, safeguarding and child protection.

Once an inspection has taken place the outcomes will be published in a report that is available for anyone to see online. The Ofsted website that holds the inspection reports has over seven million hits a month!

If schools fail an Ofsted inspection they are given 'Notice to Improve' or are put directly into Special Measures. If a school goes into Special Measures it is quite common for one of the consequences to be the Head leaving their job and the governing body being replaced.

Ofsted also has the power to act as a regulator and can grant or refuse permission for a range of services to operate. It can ensure that services meet legal requirements and has the power to deregister or even prosecute! In addition to this it can investigate parents' complaints about their school.

The Ofsted website (www.ofsted.gov.uk) tells us that Ofsted comprises a Chief Inspector, Executive Director, National Director and Regional Directors. In addition to this they have directors for Social Care, Education and Care, Children's Rights and Learning & Skills. Inspections are organised by inspection providers who are usually commercial organisations. Schools are inspected by a registered lead inspector and a team of one or more enrolled inspectors. HMIs or additional inspectors may attend the inspection when such an arrangement has been authorised. An inspection team also includes a lay inspector who has never worked in school management or educational provision.

Other parts of Ofsted's remit are to hold conferences and events for the services it inspects and to produce a wide range of publications based on its findings. Each year, in November, the Chief Inspector's report is published and its findings are based on over 45,000 inspections.

What are the merits of Ofsted?

The Office for Standards in Education has been with us since 1992, originating as part of the Conservative Party's Education Act in September 1992. It was designed to hold schools to account and to raise standards. The idea that there was a need to raise standards is an interesting one as it suggested that educational standards were in decline. The decline was allegedly due to the philosophy and practice of education that existed in schools following reports such as Plowden in 1967. This was a significant report written over three years and the first to report on education practice since the Hadow Report in the early 1930s. It is, however, very difficult to find any evidence or research that proves that there was such a decline in standards. This apparent decline in standards has been the reason for the significant government involvement in the monitoring and regulating of schools by both Conservative and Labour Parties.

Ofsted replaced the system that existed where Local Authority Inspectors and HMIs regulated and monitored schools. The change from HMI to Ofsted meant that the Secretary of State and not HMI held decision-making powers. As a result many people in the teaching profession have never seen Ofsted as a neutral organisation but as a government tool. This fact appears to have done more than almost anything to damage Ofsted's reputation amongst schools and teachers.

Inspection

Initially schools were inspected every four years for up to a week resulting in a final report more than 20 pages long (and sometimes over 40 pages long)! Since then the gap between inspections has changed frequently, increasing to every six years for schools that have previously been judged outstanding. The number of days has now decreased from up to five to two or three and there have been one-day inspections as well. The size of school will determine the number of Inspectors that are part of the inspection. The frequency and length of visits are based on perceived need. No notice inspections were introduced in 2007 and then abandoned and schools previously judged good or outstanding received one-day inspections. Inspections seem to have become shorter as data appears to dominate judgement making (some schools claim that judgements appear to have been made before the visit has taken place using data and the school's self-evaluation). In more recent years the report has reduced to only a few pages focusing and commenting on restricted areas of the curriculum, whereas initially reports commented in detail on every subject including areas like resources and accommodation.

> the frequency and length of visits are based on perceived need

The school view of Ofsted

Since 1992 schools could be described as running scared of Ofsted due to what some see as its highly political agenda. Ofsted promotes 'improvement through inspection' and many would say this maxim is one that should be looked at in some detail. Educationalists have argued that there is not enough evidence that schools have actually been helped to improve enough to justify the amount that Ofsted costs the public. For example, Ofsted's expenditure in 2007–08 was £230.5 million!

Some would argue that Ofsted has lost the confidence of many in the education system it is supposed to serve. There is a view that the conduct of school inspections varies too much and is too punitive, particularly for schools serving disadvantaged areas that many would argue are particularly subjected to unfair overall judgments as standards of attainment in limited subject areas have become of paramount importance.

At the moment there appears not to have been any serious or proper research into the evaluation of the quality and success of Ofsted's judgements of schools. Most of Ofsted's positive image appears to come from Ofsted promoting itself. In addition to this a commonly held view is that Ofsted reports can no longer be taken seriously by the teaching profession because the criteria that Ofsted uses to judge schools continually changes. In September 2010 the Education Secretary, Michael Gove, announced yet more changes to the inspection system by removing the SEF, which requires schools to rate themselves in 27 areas and reducing the areas in which schools are to be judged from seven to just four key areas: quality of teaching, leadership, pupil's behaviour and safety, and their achievements.

It has to be said that outside government and Ofsted themselves, the overwhelming view of Ofsted appears to be negative. Read the *Times Educational Supplement* each week and it is full of calls for changes to the Ofsted regime with very few supportive articles. Schools will support anything that is beneficial to their schools and the children, but they consistently knock Ofsted as do many reputable educationalists. In some schools the emphasis on test and examination scores results in staff feeling discouraged to focus on curriculum areas outside the tested areas and so some would argue that the system devalues creativity, imagination, risk taking and curriculum areas like Art, Drama, Dance, DT and Music.

The Ofsted view

Here are some Ofsted comments about successful schools that I have gathered together:

- 'Too many Headteachers are saying, "they'd like to do exciting things but" ... yet many Headteachers overcome perceived barriers and have already developed an exciting curriculum.'
- 'Well planned, motivating and broad curricula correlate with high inspection grades, high excitement and high achievement.'
- 'No good having openings, plenaries, learning objectives, success criteria if it's not an exciting curriculum and it is possible to have both.'
- 'Innovative schools often teach "the basics" in a very traditional way but then apply in an innovative way.'
- 'Memorable activities lead to memorable learning – importance of trips and visits and this is essential to the development of children.'

Ofsted in its findings also emphasises the importance of first-hand experiences, real events and activities, as well as recognising that significant learning takes place outside the classroom with genuine outcomes and purposes. Ofsted summative reports undoubtedly support good educational practice and creative exciting practice but they tend to want to see its impact on key subject areas, the tested areas. Many teachers and educational-ists would like to see non-tested areas given a higher profile and valued for their own merits and not simply for their impact on the tested subjects as some Ofsted Inspectors seem to do.

As Heads we may conclude that the negative view of Ofsted is not entirely justified but as in any organisation there are inconsistencies of approach that make an inspection unpredictable. As Heads we would hope that the Ofsted system would recognise that schools need help and support to work with all pupils, particularly those from disadvantaged areas, but the system is set up to judge, not to advise and help. A successful school is likely to see that Ofsted findings agree with the findings of their own self-evaluation. It is probably fair to say that if the system was set up to offer help and advice, albeit a more challenging brief, schools would welcome and benefit more from visits in the same way they did when HMI inspections used to operate.

Schools and self-evaluation

A school's own self-evaluation is generally a very well written and accurate analysis of the school's performance written by those who work there every day. School Improvement Partners, School Advisors and the Local Authority visit schools on a termly basis, look at the school's self-evaluation and seek evidence to support school judgements. This, it could be argued, is a successful and effective system that both judges and supports schools. The SIP and the LA are in a very good position to know and understand the school's circumstances and the challenges they face.

Earlier in this book the issue of trust was addressed and some would argue that the current inspection system is built on a lack of trust in the education system, and when this is the case it becomes counter-productive to securing the improvements that everyone, including Ofsted, wants. The wonderful thing about the education profession is that it is a caring profession; people enter it because they care about children and want to make their lives and their life chances better. Surely the government and Ofsted should take every opportunity to cherish and support that fact as openly as they can.

Some schools in disadvantaged areas do well but there is no doubt that when looking at the bigger picture, research shows that one of the biggest factors affecting educational progress is poverty and however good schools are we know that this is an issue that we cannot always address on our own. Ofsted focuses mainly on judgements based on external tests that disregard the impact of social deprivation on children's life chances and academic performance. The system is now better at recognising the different starting points pupils have in life but to accurately reflect school effectiveness a developmental and supportive inspection system is needed that helps to address the challenges such schools face. The achievement gap between 'rich and poor' will surely only be narrowed by schools and other services working together as despite all the improvements that have taken place since the advent of the national curriculum and Ofsted, this attainment/achievement gap has never been reduced. Maybe it is time to look at the inspection system and its effectiveness as well as looking at what schools are doing?

> one of the biggest factors affecting educational progress is poverty

The data: tests and league tables

There is an almost inextricable relationship between exam results and inspection judgements. Ofsted visited 6,331 primaries in 2006–07. Of these, 98% had the same inspection verdict overall as they had for 'achievement and standards'.

Ofsted's main focus is performance data when determining the quality of the school and this data covers only part of the curriculum as results only tell inspectors about the subjects tested. In primary schools it is often English and Mathematics that form the majority of the report's findings. Many argue that test and exam results may not indicate true high standards but rather how good the school is at cramming or 'teaching to the test'.

So what are the merits of Ofsted? In theory I believe it has many, and the motivation of the inspectors is to improve the life chance of children and the quality of education they receive. Where the whole system falls down in the eyes of many educationalists is in its almost exclusive focus on standards and consequently, exams, tests and league tables.

All schools must be judged and held accountable for their educational provision but whilst the system that measures that provision focuses on such a narrow area of the curriculum to make its judgements, thousands of children may suffer and fail the system because subjects like drama, dance, music, PE and sport are not given the same high profile. Just as we must never underestimate the impact we have as Heads on a school's provision neither must we underestimate the significance of Ofsted's and the government's impact on schools, dictated by their priorities.

 **case study**

Special Measures

You must look in the mirror before you look out of the window.

(Anon.)

Change is the one constant thing in education.

(Anon.)

I was Head of an Infant School and we had just received, two years running, a government award for being a school that by national standards (basically SATs results) was showing good improvement. The Junior School was in the same building, just through a pair of, historically, seldom opened double doors. I had invested considerable energy in opening lines of communication between the schools, specifically through forging a positive relationship with the long-serving Junior School Head. For Governors, the Local Authority, staff, parents and all of us in the Infant ▶

School the news that the Junior School was going into 'Serious Weaknesses' (now known as 'Notice to Improve') was a great shock. The long-standing Head retired and the almost equally long-standing Deputy Head succeeded him.

For the rest of that year nothing much changed, for the school and Governors were still in denial. I was keen, with the Local Authority, to work with the new Head who was a very experienced, well liked, respected and a very good professional. Sadly someone who I thought would have been a very good Head was thrown in at the deep end and the school was placed in Special Measures due to lack of progress.

The HMI in charge of Special Measures had visited once concluding there was a lot to do. The new Head resigned under discussion with the Local Authority and I was asked to take over running the Junior School as well as the Infant School.

'You will enjoy it, once you have taken this school out of Special Measures, you'll want to do it again with another school.' So said the Local Authority Advisor when I agreed to take on a school that was six months into the Special Measures process. She went on, 'You'll spend the first 12 to 18 months dealing with behaviour problems that will occupy most of your day … and whilst you are doing that you must get rid of those stuffed animals in the corridor … they give me the creeps!'

In Special Measures we received a termly visit from two to three HMIs to assess our progress. The HMI in charge of the process came every time with a different colleague and on the final visit brought with him the inspector who had put the school into Special Measures. Progress was significant and it was a lovely thought to ask her back so that she could see how the school had been transformed. A Governor who had outspokenly not accepted her decision to fail the school apologised to the Inspector and thanked her for putting the school into the Special Measures category saying quite simply it was the best thing that could have happened.

Special Measures provides significant support and in those days brought with it quite significant extra funding. That funding no longer exists when a school fails but it was a critical factor in moving our school forward as it was so badly resourced that tens of thousands of pounds needed spending. The school had not significantly invested in computers and I wanted at least one in each classroom, as well as an ICT suite.

One of the repercussions of a school failing seems to be staff turnover; staff blame themselves, feel like failures and often need a new start. Some staff show tenacity to help the school out of the situation for which they feel responsible before leaving. It was not many years after the school came out of Special Measures that only one member of the teaching staff remained. Some had to be encouraged to go and that is an issue, as Head, you have to be strong enough to follow through with because the need for the children to get a good education, the best that you can offer, is paramount. Schools tend not to go into Special Measures unless a significant percentage of teaching is unsatisfactory. Some staff respond to support, and improve, but others are simply unsatisfactory teachers that should have entered a different profession.

I believe we filled between 15 and 20 skips as I led the removal of out-dated equipment and resources. Old-fashioned desks were replaced with tables, ripped curtains with blinds, slate boards with whiteboards and even interactive whiteboards! Behind one of the slate boards that chalk screeched up and down on we found the signature of one of the original builders who had built the school in 1935. He had dated his signature; that board had been there a long time! I faced considerable resistance from members of the teaching staff and administrative staff unsettled by change and modernisation and reflecting on it now it must have been a very difficult time for me as Head. I was determined to transform the school and recognised I simply had to deal with each issue as it arose because the children's education was too important to avoid any of the issues. Also my credibility as a Head was on the line. I simply followed what the HMI inspector said at each visit, listed his action points and ensured they were in place by his next visit. Two other schools in Peterborough were in what we came to refer to fondly as the Special Measures Club. We all had the same Lead Inspector and he was following the same 'recipe'.

With this process, as with Ofsted inspections, I try hard to get on well with the Inspectors, try to take their advice and learn from them even if I decide to discard things they advised doing at a later date. I got on very well with the Lead Inspector and he commented very positively on how I listened, took advice and acted upon it. He was very good at his job, as I believe are most Inspectors: he got to know our school in a way that a normal inspection team never can and he cared about the school succeeding. I believe it was a matter for his pride that we did well as much as it was for me. In so many aspects of headship it is important to realise that other people often know better than you do and that their advice can benefit your school, the children and the staff.

Towards the end of the Special Measures period I had to report the Deputy Head for unprofessional conduct, deal with a deferred redundancy situation that I had inherited and anticipate what hopefully would be the visit that would take us out of Special Measures. I survived it all and the school came out of Special Measures a much better place for children to enjoy their education. I have no desire to take on another school in Special Measures!

What Ofsted look for: how to prepare for Ofsted

Historically three of the key issues that Ofsted look at are safeguarding, standards and promoting race relations, and gender equality and human rights, though with some inspections it may feel like, 'standards, standards and standards'!

Ofsted guidance

Ofsted produces excellent guidance for preparing for an inspection as well as guidance for Inspectors specific to discrete subject areas. The appropriate Ofsted handbook gives guidance relevant to a school's educational sector. Ofsted's framework for inspecting schools is another very useful document and the Ofsted website (www.ofsted.gov.uk) leads you to a plethora of documents including guidance on safeguarding, the evaluation schedule, the self-evaluation form and tackling self-evaluation.

Inspecting teams focus on the school's own self-evaluation and place a great deal of importance not only on the content but on its accuracy. Assessing the school's capacity to improve is one of the key judgements they make and the quality of leadership and management at all levels in the school comes under close scrutiny. A great deal of importance is placed upon the views of parents and pupils, and schools should have their own data and evidence in this area as part of their own self-evaluation.

Self-Evaluation

Even though a SEF was not a legal requirement and from 2011 the Ofsted SEF need no longer be completed, it is important to keep some sort of self-evaluation current in order to direct the inspection team towards what we see as our focus areas both in terms of strengths and areas for development. Prior to an inspection visit, once we have been informed that is taking place (usually in two days' time) the Head has a detailed telephone discussion with the Lead Inspector who will have devised pre-inspection briefing notes and will be substantiating their assumptions prior to arrival. In advance of the inspection the Head is asked to provide the team with the School Development Plan, school brochure, Local Authority monitoring reports, Governor minutes, school timetables and a plan of the school.

Schools are basically inspected on standards, quality of educational provision, quality of leadership and management, and the moral, spiritual, social and cultural development of the pupils at the school. Within this broad outline Inspectors look at pupils' attitudes and attendance as well as the care, guidance and support they are given to improve. The school's partnership with its community, the parents and other schools will come under scrutiny so that they

the final report identifies strengths, weaknesses and areas for improvement can provide an overall judgement on the school's effectiveness. The final report identifies strengths, weaknesses and areas for improvement.

brilliant tip

All schools are inspected within a three- to six-year period but may be inspected as soon as a year after the previous inspection. Selection for inspection is determined firstly by the date of the last inspection and then by the outcome of the last inspection, which, if it was satisfactory or worse, often results in an inspection sooner rather than later. Improving trends in performance over time or results consistently above national averages means the school is less likely to be inspected in the near future. Local Authorities meet on a regular basis with the Ofsted Regional Director to discuss local schools. If Ofsted are concerned about a school and the Local Authority agrees, finding the school is not receptive to support, then an inspection is likely in the near future. Under the current inspection system exam and test results comparisons with national averages and with similar schools are a significant determinant of when an inspection takes place.

Interviewing staff and Governors

During the inspection senior leadership team members, key subject coordinators and available Governors are interviewed. It is beneficial for the Chair of Governors and one other Governor to attend as their responses often dictate Inspectors' judgements of the effectiveness of the governing body. A Chair of Governors who visits the school regularly and is fully informed on school issues at every level can speak with great authority about the school. Allied to this is the quality of the Head's reports to Governors and the quality of Governor minutes in which governors' questions must illustrate how they hold the school to account.

Inspectors also talk to staff, pupils and others in school. No conversation is informal – do not be lulled into a false sense of security. Inspectors observe teaching and learning and as a generalisation will focus on Reception or Year 7, to assess standards on entry as well as year groups that administer standard assessment tests. It is unlikely they will observe a whole lesson but they need to observe for at least 20 minutes to make a judgement. They may also observe extra-curricular clubs, after school clubs or breakfast clubs. Senior leaders are likely to be asked to observe lessons alongside Inspectors and may even be observed feeding back to staff to check that the school's monitoring procedures are accurate.

Inspectors are very interested in tracking processes, data and its analysis. They check that performance management procedures are in place and effective, analyse samples of pupils' work and may even attend school council meetings or management meetings, but this is less likely.

Inspectors also focus on particular groups of children such as Gifted and Talented, Special Needs, English as an Additional Language or Traveller children. They may follow inspection trails to ensure, for example, that what is in a child's Individual Education Plan actually takes place, starting with the Special Needs Coordinator, then the Class Teacher, followed by the Learning Support Assistant and then the child.

Once all the evidence is gathered the inspection team simply assess how effective the school is and why.

Safeguarding

Safeguarding is not just about protecting children from deliberate harm, it includes issues for schools such as:

- pupil health and safety
- racist abuse
- use of physical intervention
- providing first aid
- educational visits
- internet safety
- school security.

- bullying
- harassment and discrimination
- meeting the needs of pupils with medical conditions
- drug and substance misuse
- intimate care
- issues which may be specific to a local area or population, for example gang activity

The Ofsted website safeguarding document gives a much fuller picture of requirements than I do here and can provide guidance and policies for staff to ensure that all who work in schools are fully aware of safeguarding procedures and expectations.

The key questions that this document advises schools to address are:

1. How safe pupils feel in school, including their understanding of issues relating to safety, such as bullying.
2. The extent to which pupils feel able to seek support from the school should they feel unsafe.
3. Pupils' own views about being safe and free from harassment.

Ofsted tells us that Inspectors will look at the extent to which children behave in ways that are safe for themselves and others, children's understanding of dangers and how to stay safe, the extent to which children show that they feel safe and are confident to confide in adults at the setting/school and the steps taken by the staff to safeguard and promote the welfare of children. In addition to this, Inspectors look at how well adults teach children about keeping safe, whether necessary steps are taken to prevent the spread of infection, and whether appropriate action is taken when children are ill. Inspectors look at the suitability and safety of outdoor and indoor spaces, furniture, equipment and toys. The maintenance of records and policies and procedures required for the safe and efficient management of the school are particularly important and the Single Central Record (SCR) is the main focus, ensuring that appropriate checks and child protection procedures are in place. The SCR also records the qualifications of the adults looking after children, so it is important that all the required data is there in an appropriate format that is recognised by your Local Authority and Ofsted (see the format on page 141 earlier).

Safeguarding also means the Inspectors will look at the effectiveness of risk assessments and actions taken to manage or eliminate risks both on the school site and with respect to off-site activities.

Equality

Another of the key areas that Ofsted has focused on is promoting race relations, gender equality and human rights, though from 2011 this area is likely to be seen as less of a priority.

The Every Child Matters agenda covered many of the issues encompassed by these areas. Basically schools must meet the needs of all pupils, encouraging them to achieve their full potential. Ofsted looks for specific actions taken by a school to tackle any differences between racial groups in terms of attainment and progress. Ofsted may compare data on different ethnic groups with respect to exclusion and attendance as well as assessment.

It is very important for schools to create a positive atmosphere where there is a shared commitment to value diversity and to respect difference. This must be integral to the ethos of the school and evident in the school office as well as in the classroom and playground. As schools we must challenge and prevent racism and discrimination and we must promote good relations between people from different racial groups. We live in a multi-ethnic society and schools must prepare children for this by promoting tolerance and understanding. Ideally a school's workforce and governing body should be representative of the community they serve, though this is not always possible as we would never prioritise such a balance over appointing the best possible person for a job.

> we must challenge and prevent racism and discrimination

The same principles apply to issues with gender equality and often, as with racism and discrimination, the battle is with the negative influence that some parents, carers and older siblings have over their children. Through assembly, PSHE and Citizenship lessons all these issues can be overtly addressed but they must permeate all that the school does and stands for. Such principles are covered within the school aims, the mission statement and within school policies but most importantly they must be evident in day-to-day practice. As Headteachers we can play a significant role here by role modelling appropriate behaviours.

Standards

The main area that Ofsted prioritises, that still seems to be its first priority in terms of determining an overall judgement, is standards. First and foremost the focus is on end of key stage assessments, tests and examinations. How does each school compare with national results and then with similar schools? Further analysis looks at value-added from the start of a key stage to the end and so an important factor to consider is the children's starting point when they enter the school. Is it well above average, above average, average, below average or well below average? Natural progression from here is to look at progress made in each year group and then to look at the progress and attainment of different groups of children beginning with investigating the difference between boys and girls and then questioning how the progress of G&T or SEN children compares with schools nationally? Other groups to analyse would be Traveller children, looked-after children and children with English as an additional language. Analysis by ethnicity will be determined by which ethnic groups make up the school population. It may also be relevant to take a look at the difference between summer-, spring- and autumn-born children.

Assessment and tracking

To address this type of scrutiny as schools we have developed robust tracking systems. Schools identify issues from comprehensive analysis of all the groups listed above and we can explain actions we have taken and their impact. Our tracking should hopefully illustrate the improvement in progress as a result of intervention programmes as well as the day-to-day teaching.

The aim of any tracking system is to illustrate an improvement in the quality of learning and teaching by showing how children's progress and attainment have improved, enabling our leadership teams to reflect on our role and the impact of our strategies. Ofsted will want evidence to prove that this is all happening. Schools usually have assessment coordinators who have an overview of the whole school, then each department, key stage, phase or subject area has someone with more in-depth knowledge of the children and their progress and finally the class teacher has the greatest knowledge of each individual's progress. All these roles in school work closely together so that a comprehensive analysis is collated, targets are set and then monitored. Findings are fed back to Team Leaders, Deputy Heads and Heads so that there is accountability at every stage.

Fischer Family Trust

A lot of schools use information from the Fischer Family Trust (FFT) to support target-setting. The FFT website (www.fischer. trust.org) describes itself as:

an independent organisation that provides a number of analyses for schools and their local authority to aid self evaluation. The FFT analyses are distributed to schools via the Assessment Support/ Professional Support Teams. In 2005, in conjunction with Ofsted, FFT developed a **'School Self Evaluation Report'** *(Analyses to Support Self Evaluation). This report was first distributed to primary and secondary schools during the 2005 Autumn Term. Ofsted Inspectors may request this report before an inspection takes place, in order for them to start drawing up hypotheses about a school's performance. The report collates data on individual pupil's performance at the end of KS2 and KS4 tests, and analyses value-added progress over a three year period; it produces an overview of trends in performance for the school and for groups within it. FFT use a contextual value-added model throughout these analyses. Reports are not provided for KS1, Infant or Special schools.*

Whatever data tracking and analysis systems we use the important thing is to be able to prove school effectiveness to Ofsted illustrating that different groups of children in different subject areas are making good progress and that strategies and interventions are having a positive impact on standards and achievement throughout the school.

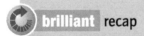 **brilliant** recap

Preparing for Ofsted is basically ensuring that, as a school, you are doing all you can to improve the life chances of children and the quality of education that they receive. It is important to read all the guidance Ofsted produces for schools and to have a very good tracking system that supports a clear and accurate self-evaluation.

When Ofsted arrives we can make sure we get the best out of the experience by getting on with the Inspectors and showing we are willing to learn from their expertise. Finally as Heads we will need to be aware of the bigger picture, to the extent of questioning the value of the inspection process. It is important that as Heads we have an opinion on such matters as the most important thing is our moral purpose and what is best for children.

CHAPTER 10

Preparing for an uncertain future

An often quoted fact is that 80% of the jobs our children will do in the future have not yet been invented. So what do we teach the children to prepare them for life? An often quoted phrase is, 'The only certainty our young people will have is uncertainty. The only thing we can predictably prepare them for is unpredictability.'

In a 21st century world where jobs can be shipped wherever there's an Internet connection, where a child born in Dallas is now competing with a child in New Delhi, where your best job qualification is not what you do, but what you know – education is no longer just a pathway to opportunity and success, it's a prerequisite for success... I'm calling on our nation's governors and state education chiefs to develop standards and assessments that don't simply measure whether students can fill in a bubble on a test, but whether they possess 21st century skills like problem-solving and critical thinking and entrepreneurship and creativity.

(President Barack Obama at the US Hispanic Chamber of Commerce, 10 March 2009)

I cannot disagree with what Obama says and sadly our key measure of assessing how well children are doing, SATs tests, is still based around 'filling in a bubble on a test'.

So what do we do? Do we anticipate what the future is going to bring and prepare and implement it ahead of time? Do we wait until someone tells us what to do? Do we wait for the bomb to drop and then clear up the mess afterwards? How visionary can we be? Are we willing to take risks? This chapter may ask more questions than it provides answers!

Technology

What are the implications of the technological revolution? Do we use mobile phones and games consoles in school? Do we allow the internet to be used by students during exams? After all, in the world we are moving into, the answer to anything that is knowledge-based can be looked up on our mobile phones!

In this context of technological advances, is school exciting enough to compete with the multi-media input children get away from school? If not what do we do about it? Will children be taught in schools and classrooms in the future? Will we need teachers or will virtual learning environments take over?

The curriculum

The most important responsibility Heads have is to ensure that children are receiving an appropriate and challenging curriculum. Are we going to maintain our current curriculum approach because it is what we have always done and because of our obsession with knowledge? Or are we going to be brave and try to ensure the curriculum is relevant to the future rather than the past? One of the biggest stumbling blocks may be people's resistance to change often based on the general view that school should be as they experienced it. Whilst educational policy is run by ministers it can be argued that it will inevitably revolve around policies that win votes. Some argue that the most significant and important decision that should be made is to remove politicians from the decision-making process with regard to educational policy.

If the most important issue for Heads to address is the relevance and appropriateness of the curriculum then how are we going to get it right for the future? When I searched on the internet for the DCSF (Department for Children, Schools and Families) under 'Schools for the Future' its website had the following to say:

We want every single child to succeed. We want every child to enjoy their childhood, to achieve their full potential and turn 18 with the knowledge, skills and qualifications that will give them the best chance of success in adult life in the 21st century. Your child, your schools, our future will help create a schools' system that provides a great start in life for every child in every school. A system that responds to the challenges of a changing global economy, a changing society, rapid technological innovation and a changing planet. A system in which every child can enjoy growing up, and which develops the potential and talents of every child and young person and gives them the broad skills they need for the future. And a system which breaks the link between deprivation, disadvantage, disability and low educational attainment and so impacts upon intergenerational poverty.

(www.dcsf.gov.uk)

As Heads we cannot really disagree with such sentiments but does the reality reflect the ambition? Some argue that our school system is still rooted in the past, in an examination and inspection system that does not prioritise the values to which the DCSF quite rightly aspires.

QCDA identified its mission as to:

develop a modern, world-class curriculum that will inspire and challenge all learners and prepare them for the future. We want the curriculum to enable all young people to become: successful learners who enjoy learning, make progress and achieve; confident individuals who are able to live safe, healthy and fulfilling lives; and responsible citizens who make a positive contribution to society.

(www.qcda.gov.uk)

As Mick Waters, the former Director of Curriculum at QCDA, said, 'The curriculum should be treasured. There should be real pride in "our" curriculum: the learning that the nation has decided it should set before its young. Teachers, parents, the wider education community, the employment community, the media and the public at large should all see the curriculum as something that they embrace, support and celebrate. Most of all, young people should relish the opportunity for discovery and achievement that the curriculum offers to them.'

Many believe that our basic school curriculum is still based on the Victorian factory model of education when children needed preparing for the implications of the industrial and agricultural revolutions and if successful within the system would go on to university. Some say that the only reason we have a six-week summer holiday is so that children could go into the fields to help bring in the crops! There is certainly no educational reason why we should have six weeks off. Below is a brief description of a typical Victorian curriculum:

Victorian lessons concentrated on the 'three Rs' – Reading, wRiting and aRithmetic. Children learnt by reciting things like parrots, until they were word perfect. The lesson was supposed to make children observe, then talk about what they had seen. Teachers found it easier to chalk up lists describing the object, for the class to copy. In addition to the three Rs which were taught most of the day, once a week the children learned geography, history and singing. Geography meant yet more copying and reciting – listing the countries on a globe.

(www.nettlesworth.durham.sch.uk/time/victorian/vschool.html)

Many schools have moved on from this but such an approach does seem to have strong similarities with SATs preparation! The danger of all the education reviews that take place is that they are so closely linked to government agendas that some would argue they never go far enough to make the radical changes that are needed.

Roses and fruit trees are trained to grow in externally pre-determined ways. Seals and other animals are trained to support set routines without error. German Shepherd dogs are trained to respond in precise ways to given stimuli. While it cannot be denied that there is a body of knowledge to be understood and skills to develop, children should not be trained: they should be educated. Children must be allowed to reflect, understand, be creative, show initiative, take risks and value their learning. Learning must not be a mechanical skill, a transmission of knowledge. We want an education system that encourages a love and joy of learning. Unsurprisingly I have yet to encounter a reflective police dog.

(Arthur, Davison and Lewis)

Some politicians, sections of the media and members of the general public hold up the mantra of 'teaching traditional subjects' as some sort of Holy Grail. The question is whether traditional subjects that go back to the 19th century are the right subjects for the 21st century. In how many other walks of life are we still following a system that was introduced over a hundred years ago? How often do we hear the business world complain that schools do not prepare children for the real world? Basically the system's success criterion is still geared to producing academics to graduate from university.

Children nowadays will watch television or listen to music whilst doing their homework and at the same time be having a social networking conversation and playing a computer game and yet the most common way of teaching children is still a basic chalk and talk, albeit pen and whiteboard, approach. Children multi-task out of choice and we teach them one thing at a time, often in silence.

What can Heads do about this 'future' dilemma when the way schools are judged still seems rooted in an examination system that measures the skills we used to need, without recognising the skills we will almost certainly need in the future?

QCDA produced their 'Big Picture' of education that aimed to help schools to develop their own, more personalised, curriculum. This overview introduced personal learning and thinking skills as well as a focus on attitudes and attributes. Both the Rose and Cambridge reviews of the primary curriculum recognised that social, emotional, creative and thinking skills are essential skills for learners and in particular for encouraging life-long learners and a love of learning. There are many initiatives worth researching that can be described as coming under the 'learning to learn' or 'inquiry-based learning' agendas. These approaches have a focus on the techniques involved in asking and answering questions so that the respondent has to think and expand upon the ideas that are generated. There is often a focus on QCDA's 'big ideas that shape the world', looking at issues like poverty, global warming, starvation and child soldiers for example. Inquiry-based learning gets away from questions that have a knowledge-based correct answer. P4C (Philosophy for Children) and Mantle of the Expert are two such initiatives, as is Open Futures. These initiatives are well worth further research as we investigate and develop a curriculum for this century, as is the work of people like Barry Hymer, Andy Hind, James Nottingham and Carol Dweck.

There are certain things we can be sure of, for example in the future we will need to work collaboratively and be team players who take risks and show initiative. A Head and a school can therefore promote and role model shared values, equality, tolerance and empathy. We can discuss what a vision of the future might look like with staff, Governors, parents and children to gain a greater understanding of a future curriculum from their perspective.

> we will need to work collaboratively and be team players

Content of the curriculum

What is important to our children as they grow up into an uncertain future? First of all the survival of the planet is a major issue for the world and, if you talk to children, a great concern to them too. Should our curriculum therefore focus on issues like global warming, the increasing world population, child soldiers and war, racism, religious differences, healthy living styles, parenting, poverty and the deprivation that exists around the world? In a world that is torn apart by wars and injustice, that is divided by different religious views, should we not be addressing these issues in the curriculum instead of basing it around knowledge, a knowledge that is available to all at the touch of a button?

I went onto Google and searched for what were considered the main issues to address in the world, and below are some of the results I found. Should these issues be the basis of our curriculum?

- survival issues like food, water, clean air
- widespread poverty in the developing world and inequalities across the globe
- climate change and its impact
- nearly a billion people entered the 21st century unable to read a book or sign their names
- less than 1% of what the world spent every year on weapons was needed to put every child into school by the year 2000 and yet it didn't happen
- some one billion children live in poverty (one in two children in the world)
- an estimated 40 million people are living with HIV/AIDS
- number of children in the world, 2.2 billion; children out of education worldwide, 121 million
- 2.2 million children die each year because they are not immunised.

Could we, should we create a curriculum around these issues and develop a nation of responsible citizens that consider others and consider issues that are important to humanity rather than a generation that may think of themselves before others? As I have said earlier in the book, as Headteachers, schools and teachers we have tremendous power and influence. If we all act together, could we change the world?

A creative curriculum

In this brave but uncertain new world we should not only be giving children the skills they will need to survive and be successful but also teaching them to be world citizens. This is where a truly creative thinking approach that focuses on the development of a skill-based curriculum centred on thinking skills such as reflection, reasoning, resilience, responsibility and resourcefulness is so important. As Alvin Toftler said: 'The illiterate of the future will not be those who cannot read and write, but those who cannot learn, unlearn, and relearn.' In an article in the *Times Educational Supplement*, Professor Bill Lucas quoted Charles Darwin from the conclusion of *On the Origin of Species*: 'it is not the strongest of the species that survive, nor the most intelligent, but the ones most responsive to change'. Children, as Darwin says, need to be adaptable, capable of managing and dealing with change. Nowadays, when change is so rapid, this ability is even more essential. Professor Bill Lucas called it 'adaptive expertise'.

If children are to succeed in the future they need to be taught that to be successful they will need both knowledge and skills like the following: cooperation, common sense, friendship, a sense of humour, integrity, caring, courage, perseverance, initiative, flexibility, effort, problem solving, curiosity, empathy, risk taking and organisation. These skills should be central to the curriculum, not peripheral and not just the prerogative of the better teachers who include them alongside a knowledge-based focus. Only then will we produce children who learn and think so that they can challenge and question not just accept, children who enjoy and love learning because they have been taught the skills to think about and understand what they are learning and children who see learning as something valuable.

If we can teach a child to learn by creating curiosity and using their imagination then surely the child is more likely to enjoy the learning process as long as he or she lives? More than ever before managing relationships and collaboration will be paramount as we move away from a world that values individual entrepreneurs above successful teams. Working with our fellow human beings from every quarter of the world will surely be the essential key to success in the future.

This is a paradigm shift in educational thinking for although schools claim to employ group work as a learning strategy more often than not it is a group of children sitting together working individually who are then ultimately tested as individuals in a testing system that is competitive and almost exclusively values an individual's score. The current testing system encourages staff to make children competitive in their learning and schools also compete with attendance data as well as academic results. Is all this competition counter-productive in the bigger picture as it is indoctrinating children to put themselves first in almost all walks of their lives?

Adaptable children should be able to work collaboratively and value it but they should also be able to compete as an individual in a running race and see the value of coming first. The problem is that there is very little in our current educational system that encourages and values collaboration and adaptive intelligence. Obviously some schools address these issues but recent history shows that any initiative or strategy to be truly valued and successful needs significant backing from government level.

At the beginning of 2010, a new decade, it was announced that government inspectors would as a priority judge schools on their ability to promote race relations, gender equality and human rights. These issues, the new legislation declared, must be judged on a par with exam results and child safety. There is some disagreement about schools having to tackle social problems at the expense of traditional education subjects but surely that depends on the content and context of that education? The curriculum of the future must surely promote equal opportunities, eliminate discrimination and ensure that stereotypical views are challenged. If it does this then it must surely also focus on major world issues.

Historically, a country's educational curriculum focused on issues and topics relevant to that country and so the historical content and the views that were propagated would generally be biased towards that country. Surely we need an education system that addresses world issues and tolerance and for younger children within a local context to make it meaningful. Some would argue that if global warming fails to destroy the world then extremist views (whether socially, religiously, ideologically or culturally based) surely will. Many countries, cities, towns and schools are multi-cultural. That is the world we live in, so surely the curriculum should be one that addresses the issues that affect humanity as a whole as opposed to having a parochial bias? Surely our curriculum must promote collaboration and adaptive intelligence if we are to move towards a world that can work together and save itself.

> we need an education system that addresses world issues

So what can a school do? What should Headteachers do?

↗ brilliant case study

A paradigm shift – creating a network of schools

In November 2003 I attended a one-day conference led by an advisor called Roger Cole called 'Building for Tomorrow'. I had already taken over Fulbridge Junior School whilst it was in Special Measures in 2001. The school came out in the summer of 2003 and was going to become a primary school in September 2004. I wanted a new curriculum direction for the school. A creative cross-curricular approach based on first-hand experiences and the local environment with a greater emphasis on the arts seemed just the ticket. This is what Roger Cole was advocating with the support of a Headteacher, Jane Loder, from Ashmead School in Aylesbury, Buckinghamshire. I was so inspired by the day and what Jane's school had achieved that I approached Roger at the end of the conference. He suggested that if there was a small group of schools in Peterborough, perhaps five or six, we could arrange a meeting with him to look at ways forward in terms of developing our curriculum approach.

I wrote to all Peterborough schools and set up a meeting at the local education centre for interested schools. We booked a room and to our amazement over 30 of Peterborough's 60 primary schools turned up! We agreed to form a group to drive curriculum change. As Roger and I left the room discussing what we could call the group we passed a drinks vending machine which gave us the name Oasis. It seemed like an appropriate name.

The next six months saw a series of meetings and conferences to inspire schools and staff into developing a creative approach to teaching the National Curriculum. Thirty three schools signed up to Oasis. Courses were put on for staff over the next two years covering a range of arts skills. Some schools developed quickly and others more slowly. Soon there was a divide being created between those schools who were keen to develop quickly and others who wanted to take a more cautious approach. It was becoming more and more difficult to cater at conferences and meetings

▶

for such a diverse range of schools. During this period Peterborough Heads visited Jane's school in Aylesbury on more than one occasion and we built links with Richard Martin from Gloucester and the work they had done developing a creative curriculum in an education action zone. The workload for me, as Head of a very large primary school in challenging circumstances, was becoming a significant issue. At this time it was agreed that we would appoint someone to manage Oasis. We appointed Di Goldsmith who had been acting-director for Arts Council East and was an Advanced Skills Teacher. The LA was approached for some financial support and we received a £2,000 one-off lump sum to use for clerical support in running the initiative.

Roger Cole and I went to the Education Show in 2006 and Roger introduced me to Mick Waters. I was so inspired by his presentation at the show that I asked if he would come and talk to Peterborough Heads. He agreed. We met the night before the conference and agreed that we wanted Mick to give Heads permission to step outside the Literacy and Numeracy strategy and look at a wider, more creative and exciting way to teach the National Curriculum. At that meal Mick proposed the idea of a Year 6 residential conference to gain the children's opinions on the curriculum, something he had wanted to do for some time. He wanted a setting with water, hills and first class hotel facilities. I agreed to organise it and said I knew just the place. Oasis would organise with QCA a residential Children's Conference to look at what children think of the current curriculum approach in schools, with the title of 'What Makes Learning Worth It?' This conference took place in mid-March at the Barnsdale Hotel, Rutland and was a significant success. Mick, almost a year later, said that it was one of the levers that led to the then current primary review.

The Children's Conference involved schools from all over the country from diverse social and economic backgrounds. Roger, Di, Mick and I invited schools we knew would be interested and five or six teachers who we knew to be excellent creative practitioners, teachers directly from the classroom. One of the teachers focused on listing skills for good learning and this steered us at Fulbridge down the line of developing creative thinkers within our arts-based, first-hand experience approach and was the trigger that moved us away from Roger's more arts-based approach to creativity.

I have maintained a good relationship with Mick Waters since that event and he was happy to support a Cultural Offer bid that was being led by Di Goldsmith and later our application to be a School of Creativity. As a school we have more recently joined the Curriculum Foundation which Mick Waters has formed since leaving QCA and has the backing of Sir Ken Robinson, Sir Tim Brighouse and Lord David Putnam.

Under Di's leadership Oasis developed significantly and the issue of schools' diverse needs was addressed through developing focus groups. Oasis developed significant links with CARA, Mathilda Joubert and the Specialist Academies Trust. The 'All Our Futures' document that preceded 'Excellence and Enjoyment' that inspired our approach is still in my view one of the key documents for curriculum development for the future.

With respect to Fulbridge School we developed our own unique approach to the curriculum and the school environment. This has led to many Peterborough schools visiting us as well as schools and visitors from much further afield to look at our environment and curriculum. We were determined not to buy an 'off the shelf – one size fits all' scheme as we felt this would not be a truly creative approach to designing the curriculum and did not simply want a cross-curricular approach. We wanted to create something original and of value, that suited our school, our children, our staff, our locality and our building. We wanted a curriculum that focused on skills that the children would need in the future and so we based it around creative thinking skills, that we termed Life skills, Knowledge-based skills and Physical skills (see Figure 10.1)

Our distinctive approach has now led to me visiting colleges of further education to talk to students about our creative curriculum approach and the work of Oasis including our links with QCA and the focus on the 'Pupil Voice'. I have spoken to G&T coordinators in Bedfordshire and Norfolk as well as talking annually to students at Homerton College in Cambridge and Bishop Grosseteste College in Lincoln. I have spoken at the Education Show, led two seminars at the London Institute of Education and led a seminar with all the Heads and staff in Guernsey. I see this as an opportunity to have a wider impact and to influence others to consider the

▶

KEY SKILLS FOR BECOMING A CREATIVE THINKER AT FULBRIDGE SCHOOL **(Based on the QCA model)**				
Functional Skills Academic/Curriculum/Subject Specific	**Personal, Learning and Thinking Skills**			
	Life Skills	Creative Thinking Skills	Physical Skills	ICT Skills
Literacy	Cooperation	Questioning	Coordination	Using a spreadsheet
Numeracy	Common sense	Challenging	Flexibility	Taking photographs
ICT	Friendship	Making connections	Speed	Filming
Science	Sense of humour	Seeing relationships	Agility	Data processing
Geography	Integrity	Envisaging what might be	Balance	Gathering, storing and retrieving information
History	Caring	Exploring ideas	Control	Presentation of ideas
Music	Initiative	Reflection	Endurance	Use a variety of ICT tools
DT	Flexibility	Imagination	Spatial Awareness	Safe use of the internet
Art	Effort	Enquiry	Strength	Communication of information
Drama	Courage	Risk taking	Fluency	Publishing
Dance	Problem Solving	Working collaboratively/negotiation	Harmony	Animation
RE	Curiosity		Precision	Musical presentations
PSHE/Citizenship	Perseverance		*Taken from the SAQ (speed, Agility, Quickness) programme*	Finding, classifying and checking accuracy of information
Photography and Filming	Organisation			
PS (see 'Physical Skills')		*Explorers, Judges, Warriors, Inventors*		
Tools to use:	Philosophy for Children, P4T, Brain Gym, PMIs, Thinking Hats, Mind Maps, VAK, SAQ, Jabadeo, Mantle of the Expert			

Functional Skills: The core elements of English, Mathematics and ICT that provide individuals with the skills and abilities they need to operate confidently, effectively and independently in life, their communities and work.

Personal, Learning and Thinking Skills: (http://curriculum.qca.org.uk)
Six groups of skills:
• Independent enquirers
• Creative thinkers
• Reflective learners
• Team workers
• Self-managers
• Effective participants

Each curriculum area needs a list of discrete 'functional skills'; especially English, Mathematics and ICT.

Figure 10.1 Key skills for becoming a creative thinker

Source: Adapted from Big Picture of the Curriculum by The Qualifications and Curriculum Development Agency (www.qcda.gov.uk)

benefits of a creative approach to teaching our National Curriculum and to promote liaison between schools.

Schools within Oasis also worked with CARA as part of an action research project. At the time it involved more schools in one combined piece of action research than CARA had ever worked with. This was a fantastic learning journey for all staff involved as we explored ways in which movement and expressing your feelings through exploration and movement can impact on writing.

In 2009 it became apparent that the Oasis project manager post that Di Goldsmith held could no longer be sustained as school budgets in the economic downturn were very tight and schools were reluctantly pulling out of paying the subscription. For a network to last almost six years with little or no financial or Local Authority support is quite remarkable and the legacy of Oasis on schools in Peterborough is highly significant. Had the cultural bid been successful then we would have extended Oasis' life and embarked upon our aim of bringing together the educational sector and the cultural sector to develop a Peterborough Creative Curriculum based around what Peterborough has to offer: Flag Fen, the Cathedral and Museum, Ferry Meadows, the Nene Valley railway, the River Nene etc.

Towards the end of Oasis we read about the opportunity to apply to be a National School of Creativity through Creative Partnerships. This seemed an opportunity to further develop our creative journey and the collaboration we had enjoyed with other schools. After an extensive self-analysis and a thorough external assessment we were one of only 26 schools in 2009 to be awarded this status.

Through these collaborations we have learnt how much more there was to learn from experts and other schools to enrich and advance our creative journey. A journey that will never end … and nor do we want it to.

It has also been a significant learning curve for staff, which has resulted in many collaborations with other schools, not just locally but from across the whole country, and was indeed a paradigm shift in our educational practice.

brilliant recap

The world is changing fast: many of today's most popular graduate jobs did not exist 20 years ago. It will continue to change fast and unpredictably, so today's young people will need to be able to learn and re-train, think and work in teams and to be flexible, adaptable and creative. They also need to develop a sense of responsibility for themselves, for their health, for their environment, and for their society. They need to develop respect and understanding for those from different backgrounds, and the confidence and skills to make a positive contribution to their community.

(www.dcsf.gov.uk)

How right DCSF are. So should the Ofsted system and the examination system be radically changed to value and reflect the DCSF aspirations? Perhaps it is already changing, but slowly. Perhaps the 'traditional subjects' and 'back to basics' lobby are so strong that politically it is too sensitive an issue to radically change what has existed for over a century. Changing may lose votes and whilst the education system and curriculum depends on politicians making the decisions, it could be argued those decisions will always be dictated by voters and the media. Is it right that our children's educational futures are dictated by columnists and politicians rather than the professionals and the educationalists? Or is this view too cynical? One thing is for sure, as a Head, the most important aspect of our job is to get the curriculum we lay before the children appropriate for the children in our schools.

In America a conference was set up to look at 'Teaching, Learning and Applying 21st Century Skills' for teachers, administrators, teacher-educators, and education policy makers. The Conference's purpose was not only to enhance awareness of the skills and ways of thinking students will need in order to meet and successfully address the multiple challenges of the 21st century, but also – and most importantly – to provide strategies and share examples of how to incorporate these skills into curriculum and teaching. The conference was based around these core questions:

- What are 21st century skills?
- Why do students need to learn them?
- Does teaching 21st century skills impact the teaching of basic knowledge?
- How do teachers teach so that their students learn these skills?
- What is the teaching-learning environment in which these skills are learned?
- What technologies can be incorporated and how can they best serve as catalysts and tools?
- How do we assess students?
- What is productive problem solving (PPS) and how can it be incorporated into teaching and learning for the 21st century?
- How can students reflect on and effectively communicate their process and actions to others?

These questions seem like a good starting point for any Headteacher or aspiring Headteacher to address if we want to prepare our students for an uncertain future.

CHAPTER 11

The best job in the world

Headship has been described as the best job in the world; I think it is exciting and rewarding in a way that is unlike any other job and I hope that this book has encouraged those who are in education to aspire to become a Head. I have written about the areas of responsibility that a Head has, what Heads actually do and the challenging aspects of the job. However three themes have dominated the book: firstly that headship should be more about leading than managing, without understating the issue of managing a school well; secondly that the type of curriculum that we as Heads and our schools set before the children in our schools is of paramount importance; and thirdly the whole issue of what factors make a good Headteacher. Leading a school in times of change is also a major test for any new Heads, but as is evident in Chapter 2, Heads are better prepared for the job nowadays than ever before.

The curriculum

'All Our Futures: Creativity, Culture and Education' was a major report on the future of education and one that many people would say has not been heeded enough by decision makers despite the government continually emphasising that education is a top priority. Educationalist B. F. Skinner once said: 'Education is an important function of a culture – possibly in the long run it's the most important or only function.' What is puzzling is why, when almost all educational thinkers support a different focus for education other than exams and tests, we still continue with a system that some would argue actively harms children's development. Is it simply our obsession with the past and traditional subjects or is it that politicians want a system that they can quantifiably measure?

Read any educational theorist going back to Piaget, Bruner, Vygotsky and in more recent times John Holt, Benjamin Bloom, Sir Ken Robinson, Professor David Hargreaves, Andy Hargreaves, Guy Claxton, Howard Gardner, Professor John MacBeath, Sir Tim Brighouse, Professor Mick Waters … the list is endless, and you will find they have one thing in common – disagreement with the philosophy behind our current educational system and the curriculum focus that it inevitably has due to the way it is measured and reported. How well a school is doing seems to have become synonymous with SATs results, GCSE results and A Level results, particularly with respect to English and Mathematics. An outstanding school is a school that gets good exam results, or so it seems.

Under the current system any real change needs government action and backing. 'All Our Futures' was commissioned by the government and reported back to the Secretary of State. The report is in response to the challenge that faces education with the economic, social and technological changes that are taking place worldwide. The report advocates radical changes with a much greater emphasis on creative and cultural education. It describes how we live in a country where the manufacturing industry has been superseded by creative industries and where academic qualifications no longer guarantee you a job, yet we still have an education system that has not really changed its aspirations for over a hundred years. This book has emphasised that Heads of today and the future must make sure that the curriculum is relevant to today's children and their futures for the appropriateness of the curriculum is a Head's biggest responsibility. As the 'All Our Futures' report emphasises, schools must respond to the economic, technological, social and personal development challenges of today's world. This makes a Head's job exciting and such a significant one in its importance.

But why make such a radical change? I believe it was summed up very well by Sir Ken Robinson in an article in the *Times Educational Supplement*:

The problem lies in our education system, which was developed in the 19th Century to meet the needs of industrialisation and is based on the principles of manufacturing and the intellectual culture of universities. We need a radically different sort of education for the 21st Century, as our children face challenges that are without precedent.

(Ken Robinson (2009) 'Reach for the Michelin stars, not McSchools', TES, 3 July)

Creativity

Many argue that we need a national strategy for creativity. You can be creative at anything that involves your intelligence but it is hard to be creative within an education culture that is obsessed with standardisation. You cannot promote innovation and creativity in a culture that values a single answer.

All the great schools in Britain are great for the same reason, not because of standardisation, but because they are customised to their children, their circumstances, their teachers and their community.

Bernard Barker has written a book called *The Pendulum Swings: Transforming School Reform* in which he challenges the government's five main assumptions about successful schools and school leadership. He challenges the notion that a 'super-Head' can transform any school into being a highly successful school, that schools can overcome social disadvantage and improve life chances, that free market competition improves quality, that central regulation backed up by continuous inspection improves schools and that adopting 'best practice' recommendations will transform a school's performance. Bernard Barker concludes that there is an urgent need to abandon the government's current approaches to improving education and to establish a new progressive vision of education. Whether he is right or wrong it is probably safe to say that in the future the focus of current government policy, the functional, knowledge-based skills will change and due to developments in ICT may become redundant, whereas the social and emotional skills such as collaboration, flexibility, curiosity, reflection, negotiation and perseverance will always be essential ingredients in making a person successful. The message from this, for us as Heads, is not to always accept the status quo; we must challenge, question and seek out what is the best for our pupils and our school communities.

> we must challenge, question and seek out what is the best

What makes a good Headteacher?

The need to be innovative and creative with the curriculum links to one of the most important qualities of successful headship – that of having a clarity of vision about achieving what is important for our schools. As Heads we must surely have the courage to focus on realising the school's vision and be unremitting in our efforts to do what is best for the children in our care.

Sir Tim Brighouse says that good Heads stalk the corridors, lead inspiring assemblies and are always accessible to staff and pupils. Successful Heads are charismatic without being overpowering and can encourage leadership in others so that even the youngest pupil or member of staff feels comfortable making decisions and offering ideas. There are contradictions here though as we must ask whether the Head's role is now more like that of a business leader than an educationalist. In my view combining both these aspects of the job is not just a challenge but what makes the job so exciting and rewarding. As Heads we certainly have become more entrepreneurial and we may not be necessarily Head 'teachers' any more, maybe more of a Head 'of School'. Headship is about having a clear focus on our school's goals, about challenging under-performance and ensuring good value for money and high educational standards. As the book has emphasised, a Head must also be someone who retains a positive outlook, no matter what challenges are being faced. A Head must be an emotionally intelligent person who is empathetic towards all over whom they have influence, for if they are not they can become self-absorbed and unaware of what their school community really wants and needs. If as Heads we become consumed in our own self-importance and forget that our main purpose is to serve our school community then we are likely to fail in the job of Headship.

Successful Heads have a strong moral purpose, they put others first and have a strong set of personal values that are shared with and responsive to the school community. In addition to this, as Heads, we must have passion and a strong desire to achieve excellence whilst creating a community that has a strong sense of unity and trust. As Heads we aspire to get the best out of others, we are enablers, we nurture and develop, we allow others to take credit whilst strategically taking the blame on our shoulders when things do not go well so that our schools move ever forward.

As each new school year approaches there is the joy of making decisions about the school curriculum, welcoming back all the pupils, sorting out staffing arrangements, welcoming the Newly Qualified Teacher who is excited about their first job and class, and working alongside dedicated and enthusiastic staff. As Heads we never know what each day will bring. When we need some inspiration one avenue I have tried to advocate is the 'rebel with a cause' approach that can be achieved by creating something that challenges the educational status quo but in doing so benefits the children in our care.

As far as the future is concerned I am generally optimistic as there are undoubtedly a higher percentage of both teachers and Headteachers in the system who are more highly qualified, focussed, trained and committed than ever before. This is due, in no small part, to the unprecedented amount of money and support that education has received since the 1990s. Where schools put effective children's learning at the heart of all they do, where a curriculum approach is developed that is tailor-made to each individual school's needs then the life chances of children are significantly enhanced. After all, we all came into education to primarily improve children's lives.

As Heads we must believe that we can give staff and pupils the roots so that they can grow wings and fly!

Further reading

Barker, Bernard (2010) *The Pendulum Swings: Transforming School Reform*, Stoke on Trent: Trentham Books

Brighouse, Professor Tim *Essential Pieces: the Jigsaw of a Successful School* and *How Successful Head Teachers Survive and Thrive*, www.rm.com

Cole, Roger (2006) *The Creative Imperative*, Lichfield: Primary First

Covey, Dr Stephen R. (1990) *The Seven Habits of Highly Effective People*, New York: Free Press

Covey, Dr Stephen R. (2006) *The Speed of Trust*, New York: Free Press

Craft, A. (2005) *Creativity in Schools: Tensions and Dilemmas*, Abingdon: Routledge

Dweck, C. S. (2006). *Mindset: The New psychology of success*, New York: Random House

Hargreaves, Andy (2009) *The Fourth Way: The Inspiring Future for Education Change*, Thousand Oaks: Corwin Press

Heifetz, Roland (1994) *Leadership Without Easy Answers*, Belknap: Harvard University Press

Hymer, Barry (2009) *Gifted & Talented Pocketbook*, Alresford: Teachers' Pocketbooks

Robinson, Ken (2001) *Out of Our Minds: Learning to be Creative*, Wiley-Capstone

Robinson, Ken (2009) *The Element: How Finding Your Passion Changes Everything*, London: Viking

Strickland, Bill (2007) *Make the Impossible Possible*, New York: Broadway Books

Index